INSPIRATION FOR
CHRISTIAN TEEN GIRLS

INSPIRATION FOR CHRISTIAN TEEN GIRLS

A Weekly Devotional and Journal

Katara
Washington
Patton

**ROCKRIDGE
PRESS**

Interior Designer: Jen Cogliantry
Cover Designer: Suzanne LaGasa
Art Producer: Sara Feinstein
Editor: Adrienne Ingrum
Production Editor: Andrew Yackira
Production Manager: Holly Haydash
Illustrations used under license from Creative Market

ISBN: Print 978-1-64152-850-4 | eBook 978-1-64152-851-1

I DEDICATE THIS BOOK TO MY DAUGHTER, KAYLA. MAY GOD GUIDE YOU THROUGH YOUR

TEEN YEARS, AS WELL AS ALL OF

THE YEARS YOU HAVE ON EARTH.

I LOVE YOU—MAMA.

THIS JOURNAL BELONGS TO

Madee-Rae Hazel

CONTENTS

TEEN SPIRIT

Life as a teen girl can be fun and thrilling. It can also bring about difficult emotions and tricky situations. But don't worry; there's help. When I was a teenager, my mom told me the Bible is a road map for life. I didn't fully get it, or believe her. But as I grew up I got to know God and the Bible, and I learned she was right. The problem had been that the Bible isn't an easy read. I needed help to understand what its words meant and how they applied to my life.

That's one reason I write for teens. If you "get" the Bible now, you'll grow stronger in your relationship with God. That can totally change your life, helping you face each day with confidence, knowing God has your back.

This devotional journal makes it easy to get closer to God by dividing the Word into just-the-right-size portions. It explains some of those confusing passages in God's Word and how they're applicable to your life right now. (Yes, the Bible speaks to teen girls today, even though it is thousands of years old.)

You will find words of encouragement, inspiration, and wisdom on every subject imaginable—from fashion, to bullies, to social media, to friends, and more. You'll see words from scripture but also see plain language that is easy to understand. You can relate the Word of God to your situation, using the activities and questions designed for personal reflection. You can write down your thoughts, or even record them, and think about the theme throughout the week.

I've heard that teens feel it's a lot of pressure to have a new devotion every day. Not to worry! Just read and journal about one Bible passage each week to help you focus on *you*, grow closer to God, and become a better friend and person. There are 53 devotions—just enough for one a week for an entire year. You can start any day of the year. And there's probably no better day than today.

The sample prayer at the end of each devotion is there to help you talk to God; fill in your own words or say the prayer as it is to start the conversation.

Enjoy using this book as a tool to learn more about God, the Word, and how it can be helpful in every decision you make. Let it change your world and show you the life God uniquely designed you to live.

You might also use this devotional to spark discussions with your family members and friends. Do the activities together and share your outcomes.

Happy growing!

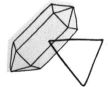

Bible Quotations

You don't need a Bible to enjoy this book. Each of the 53 devotions includes a quotation from the Bible, so you don't need to look up anything!

But if you *do* have a Bible, a Bible app, or access to the Internet, that's even better. Many Bible apps are free. Search "Bible" in an app store on your phone, tablet, laptop, or computer. You'll discover more choices than you can imagine. Many church websites also include Bibles.

The Bible is a compilation of 66 books. When you check out the contents page of a Bible, you'll see the list of those books starts with Genesis and ends with Revelation.

Each book of the Bible is divided into **chapters**.

Each chapter is divided into **verses**.

Scripture references are made by book, chapter, and verse. For example, Genesis 2:4 means the book of Genesis, chapter 2, verse 4.

Sometimes letters appear after the reference. For example, Genesis 2:4 (NIV). Those letters refer to the **translation** of the Bible—New International Version, in this case.

The Bible is an ancient book. It was not originally written in English. It has been translated for those of us who read English. Many, many translators have put these ancient words into our language. And just like you might say "Hello," "Hi," "Howdy," "Yo," "Hey," "Whassup," or some other greeting, different translators choose different words to convey the meaning of these ancient languages. This book uses various Bible translations in hopes that you will easily understand what God is saying in each scripture quoted. You'll find the list of translations used on pages 147–148.

I Can Do Hard Stuff

Life can be tough sometimes; it can be hard, harsh, and even brutal. Realizing that is a big part of growing up. But your faith can be particularly helpful when you encounter challenges—from schoolwork, to difficult family situations, to everything in between.

Faith is not only believing that God exists. Faith is believing that the Almighty has the ability to help you overcome tough times and endure hard things. You may not be able to figure out just how God can help, or when the Lord will come through, but you can use faith to trust that God will.

Reviewing scripture can encourage you, too. The Bible is filled with evidence of God's miracles at times when things just seemed impossible. Recalling and reflecting on how other people handled their situations can provide strength and inspiration.

In Mark, Jesus tells his disciples that "all things are possible with God" (10:27). The rough stuff. The challenging things. The difficult and insurmountable. God can help you get through it.

When you pray and trust God, the Holy Spirit can give you ideas, perhaps ways to handle your situation: whether studying with a tutor if you're struggling in calculus, finding a counselor for a problem at home, or learning to break a big task into small to-dos so you can handle it better. And then God can add the supernatural power to push you over the hump and get you where you want to be. You may not see how, but activate your faith and trust God. With God, it is possible.

> Jesus looked at them and said, "With man this is impossible, but not with God; all things are possible with God."
>
> Mark 10:27 (NIV)

Read 2 Kings 4:1-7. How did God use Elisha to help the widow who was in debt?

He had the Sons get the oil Then sell it to pay off your debt.

Record or write down situations that feel hard or impossible. Spend time praying about these items and jot down, or record, any thoughts that come to mind.

Online school, Saying to my grammy that i don't want to see her, Opening up, period

Throughout the week, look for ways God has done the impossible. Ask people you know and listen to their stories. Reflect on how these stories can help you trust that God can do the impossible in your situation.

DEAR GOD . . .

I need your help with Understanding more things in life.

Show me how to handle this tough situation. Strengthen my faith in you as I wait for your assistance. Amen.

God Knows Me

It's easy to feel like you don't matter. You're just one person among billions of others. How many people actually know you—your name, what you like, what makes you tick, and what makes you upset? At times you may wonder whether you truly know yourself as you grow and change.

But there's someone who understands you better than you could imagine. God. In fact, God is aware of every detail: what you like, what scares you, and what you desire. And God knows just how many hairs are on your head. Yes, God really knows you.

So, when you are searching for a connection, hoping to share with someone who gets you, try God. You can talk to God just like you talk to your best friend. You don't have to use any formal language. Even when you can't think of what to say, God can understand your groans and moans—the wordless sounds you make (see Romans 8:26).

> Are not two sparrows sold for a penny? Yet not one of them will fall to the ground apart from your Father. And even the hairs of your head are all counted. So do not be afraid; you are of more value than many sparrows.
>
> Matthew 10:29-31 (NRSV)

You can find comfort in knowing God cares so much about you and knows so much about you. You don't have to walk alone in this big world. You can walk with God, assured that God gets you. And if there's something you don't like about yourself, take it to God. Perhaps it's the way you're supposed to be, and God will help you accept yourself. Or if it is a bad habit or trait, God can also help you change. Trust God; after all, your Creator knows you best.

Celebrate the fact that God knows you. Write or record five things you love about yourself. Write or record two things you'd like to change about yourself. Thank God for knowing all about you.

That I'm always nice, feels good, cares about others, trys hard, acepts everyone; Im not that pretty, Im allways trying to look better

Write a letter to God sharing how it feels to be known so intimately. Use the letter to help you open up to God. Read your letter each day this week and consider adding to it.

Dear god, I try to get better at everything I want to try to get better at not doing that.

HI, GOD

I'm so grateful to know that you truly get me. I want to share more with you and grow closer to you. Help me to feel more coFident about me and my body.

Using My Gifts

God has given everyone gifts so that we all give back to others, so that we too contribute to the world. An artist shares beauty. An athlete helps build pride in a school, city, region, or country. A teacher inspires. A talented writer informs and entertains.

Some have discovered and developed their gifts, while others are still wondering. You might be asking yourself: What am I good at? What do I do well? What can I contribute to the world?

All talents can be used to help others. But if we don't use our talents, danger awaits. Check out the Parable of the Talents in Matthew 25:14-30. A parable is a story that uses an everyday example to make a spiritual point. In this parable, Jesus uses an investor who goes on a trip and the people he leaves in charge of his money to illustrate what we should do with our gifts. Most Bibles use the word "talent," which is what "a thousand dollars" might mean in biblical times. The people who had five and two talents used them to make more money. But the person who only had one talent hid what had been entrusted to him. He may have been trying to keep it safe, or he could have been too lazy to do anything.

When the investor returned, he was pleased with those who doubled their talents, but he was angry with the person who gave him back the one talent. Our gifts are like the talents. God entrusts us with gifts and we are to share them with the world.

For to everyone who has, more will be given, and he will have abundance; but from him who does not have, even what he has will be taken away.

Matthew 25:29 (NKJV)

God doesn't want you to waste—or hide—what you've been given. Girls are sometimes taught to hide what we are good at, to not do as well as we can in order to let boys do best, or to just help men contribute to the world. That's hiding our talents.

List ten of your talents, gifts, or skills. Next to each one, note how you can use it.

1. Caring - I can care for people

2. Loving -

3. Respectful -

4.

5.

6.

7.

8.

9.

10.

This week, read different versions of Matthew 25:14-30. If you don't have different versions of the Bible, go online or use a Bible app. You can get many different versions of this parable.

How does this parable inspire you to develop your gifts and use them?

GOD, GIVER OF ALL GOOD GIFTS

Show me what you've given me to use to inspire, inform, or help others. I want to develop my gifts and skills, and use them for good. Amen.

I Can Forgive

If you were to take an informal survey among the Christians you know and were to ask them to name one of the toughest things to do as a follower of Christ, one response would be high on the list: forgive.

To forgive means to excuse another person's behavior when that person has wronged you. It's saying I can let this go and move on.

Forgiveness seems hard at first. You are stuck thinking about the harm or feeling the emotions stirred up from the incident. A bestie shared a secret, a loved one betrayed you, or someone hurt you on purpose. These things can sting—big time. But how can you follow God's example and forgive?

The king summoned the man and said, "You evil servant! I forgave your entire debt when you begged me for mercy. Shouldn't you be compelled to be merciful to your fellow servant who asked for mercy?" The king was furious and put the screws to the man until he paid back his entire debt. And that's exactly what my Father in heaven is going to do to each one of you who doesn't forgive unconditionally anyone who asks for mercy.

Matthew 18:32-35 (MSG)

The Parable of the Unforgiving Servant found in Matthew 18:21-35 can help. As you read the story, it might make more sense to think of it in modern terms. Let's say you owe a friend one hundred dollars. It is time to pay up, but you don't have the one hundred dollars. When you let your friend know you can't quite make your payment yet, she says: "That's okay; I'll let it go. Don't worry about paying me back at all." That's great news! Think how you'd feel!

But then a friend to whom you loaned ten dollars comes and lets you know she's in the same situation that you were in; she doesn't have the money right now to pay you back. What do you think you'd do?

If you're starring in the parable, you'd yell and scream at your friend. You'd berate her for not keeping her word and paying back your ten dollars when she said she would. You would ask her how she could betray you and not live up to her word! Your words would punish her.

Do you see the irony here? One friend let you off the hook, but you're unable to do the same?

What does this have to do with forgiveness? It all comes back to how God has treated us, believers in Jesus Christ. God has forgiven us for everything we do wrong; therefore, God expects us to forgive others for wrongs done to us. It's a cycle. We receive God's forgiveness, and we freely share forgiveness with others. When we remember the cycle of forgiveness, it can make it a lot easier to let stuff go. When we focus on the way God treats us, it becomes possible to release the anger and pain caused by others. Yes, we need ways to prevent people from continuously hurting us, but when they do, we can still forgive them and stop holding on to the hurt.

Whom do you need to forgive?

i need to learn how to forgive
My grandmother Dawn.

Every day this week, write or record one thing God has forgiven you for or one thing you want God to forgive you for. Pray over this list as you ask God for forgiveness.

MERCIFUL LORD

Thank you for forgiving my debt. I know you want me to do the same and forgive others when they hurt me. Help me forgive

My Grandmother Dawn.

Heal my pain and help me let it go. In Jesus' name. Amen.

I Choose to Be Smart

To be smart or to use wisdom may sound like something you aspire to when you're much older, when you're counting your gray hairs and sharing lessons from your long life. But really, wisdom is a virtue that can help you out right now—and for the rest of your life.

Think about it: To be smart or wise means to make good choices based on knowledge or experience. Wisdom is like an inner compass that guides you and leads you to the best decisions. Isn't that something you could use in your life right now? Wisdom can help you choose friends, the best classes, and the best places to hang out—or where not to hang out!

In 1 Kings, God gave King Solomon the opportunity to ask for anything he wanted. And Solomon chose to ask God for wisdom. Solomon wanted wisdom to know the difference between right and wrong so that he could rule the people.

Solomon's request was so wise that God not only granted him wisdom, but God gave Solomon riches and respect, too (see 1 Kings 3:5-14). Wisdom definitely has its benefits. Good things happen when you make smart choices.

Do you want to know right from wrong and be empowered to make the best choices for your life? God wants that for you, too, and promises to give you wisdom if you only ask for it. When you ask, be genuine and sincere; don't fake it. God knows the difference. Open your heart up to the Lord and ask for wisdom to know the difference between right and wrong. Ask specifically for the answers you need and wait for God to point you in the right direction. You may feel peace about a certain decision, or you may feel drawn a certain way. Follow wherever God leads you and know that your choices will lead to what is best.

If any of you need wisdom, you should ask God, and it will be given to you. God is generous and won't correct you for asking. But when you ask for something, you must have faith and not doubt. Anyone who doubts is like an ocean wave tossed around in a storm.

James 1:5-6 (CEV)

Write down or record the things you need wisdom and direction about right now. Pray about them each day this week.

School, Basketball, ElA . i need
help with these because School
is hard and i want to get better
at all of these

The book of Proverbs is a collection of wise sayings and contains exactly 31 chapters. If you read one a day, you can cover the entire book in one month. Start by reading the chapter that matches today's date (for example, if it is the fifth of the month, read Proverbs 5). Try reading one chapter each day this week. You may want to continue until you've read all 31.

HOLY GOD

I want to make the right decisions. Give me the wisdom to know what is best. Right now, I need direction about School
and basketball.

I trust and believe that you will guide me in the right way. I am grateful that you provide wisdom when I ask. Amen.

Attitude Check

Have you ever been told to check your attitude? Or to *watch* your attitude? It might sound silly to think of an attitude as something you have to pay close attention to, but it can make a big difference in a situation. How you see something or your thoughts toward someone can shape how you act or even influence the results, or outcome, of the circumstances.

For example, you might not want to go on a family outing. You'd much rather stay home and talk on the phone with your friends. But your mom insists you come. Maybe your mind becomes fixed on not wanting to go and all of the things you'd rather not, but are going to have to, do with the family. Those things become dumber and dumber to you in your mind because you just don't want to do them. So of course, when you do them, you don't enjoy them, and you have a terrible time out with your family.

What if you could change your attitude—the way you are thinking—about the outing? You have more power than you might think over your feelings. Instead of being miserable, you could send a quick message to your friends letting them know you'll be available later, and then think about some of the ways you enjoy your family. You could review the good things about each member, like how happy your mom gets when you spend time together, your dad's embarrassing jokes, or your brother's ability to beat everyone at games. Then you'll be happier about that family outing—even if you still can't wait to get home to chat with your friends.

> God blesses those people who depend only on him. They belong to the kingdom of heaven! . . . God blesses those people who are humble. The earth will belong to them!
>
> Matthew 5:3-5 (CEV)

What you think, what you hold in your mind, often impacts whether things turn out negatively or positively. That's why checking your attitude often can help you adjust a situation when needed. It can get you in the right frame of mind.

Jesus listed a set of behaviors that we call the Beatitudes in Matthew 5. He said that people are blessed, or happy, when they have these types of attitudes. Check out ways you, too, can be happier when your attitude is right.

Each day this week, write or record a description of your attitude. Choose an emoji that best fits your attitude and draw it next to your description.

_____

_____

_____

If you're having a tough time doing something you don't want to do, check your attitude. Review Matthew 5:3–11. Which Beatitude would help you have a better attitude about your situation?

DEAR GOD

Help me have a better attitude about _____.
Give me the right perspective so that I feel blessed and happy.
Show me how to think more positively, like you want me to
think. Amen.

I Am Beautiful

What do you see when you look in the mirror? Do you see the beautiful young woman God created, or do you see imperfections and things you'd like to change? It can be tough growing up in today's comparison culture and dealing with all of the (normal!) changes happening with your body. You may think you're not beautiful unless you're shaped like that model in a jeans ad, or unless you have lips like the stars on Instagram. But the truth is, a lot goes into creating the images that the media projects as ideal or beautiful. And you can't perfect perfection! You were created by God to be just as you are now—and Psalm 139:14 says you are marvelous.

Think about it for a moment: God, the creator of the world, took the time to make you. Your Creator molded together the parts of your body when you were in your mother's womb to form the person you are. God made you wonderful and complex. Unique and spectacular. God did that.

If you don't feel beautiful and wonderful, take a closer look in the mirror (or inside your heart). Ask yourself why you don't see what God created. Are you allowing your desire to look like someone else to cloud your vision and prevent you from seeing what God created? Beauty goes way beyond what meets the eyes. Your inner being matters more than your outward appearance. And what you feel about yourself inside will show up on the outside. So, if you're not feeling like a fabulous creation of God, check inside to see what's going on. Do you believe God created you? Do you believe God would make you less than marvelous?

> You made all the delicate, inner parts of my body and knit me together in my mother's womb.
>
> Thank you for making me so wonderfully complex! Your workmanship is marvelous—how well I know it.
>
> Psalm 139:13-14 (NLT)

Yes, taking care of your external body can help you look great—things like beauty routines, exercise, and healthy eating can be fun and go a long way. But what's inside of you will set the tone for what you see and what you project to others. Nourish your inner being, thank God for creating you, and celebrate all the amazing things your body helps you do—instead of simply concentrating on how it looks. When you do these things, your perception begins to change. Your marvelousness is right in front of your eyes. Take a look.

Record or write below all of the things you think are marvelous about your inner self and your outer self. Review your list this week.

Inner self   **Outer self**

MIGHTY CREATOR

Thank you for creating me specially and for loving whom you made. I will continue to praise you for making me the unique person I am throughout my life. Amen.

Why Am I Depressed?

Depression is a tricky emotion. It can creep up on you, make you not want to do any of the things you enjoy, and distort your thinking. Depending on the level of your depression, you may feel worthless or like you cannot focus. And depression can range from feeling a little down or blue to not wanting to get out of bed, or worse, perhaps wanting to harm yourself. Depending on how badly you feel and for how long, you may need outside help. Don't be afraid or ashamed to get it. Talk to your parents, a trusted counselor, or someone else who can point you in the direction of help.

Depression can be caused by a variety of things—some within your control. But most of the causes are out of your control. Your hormones, how you're treated by a peer, or a tragic event can trigger depression. Sometimes, even what you eat can cause you to feel down or not like yourself. It's important to remember that depression doesn't mean you are bad or worthless. It means you need help to treat your emotions—especially, according to many experts, if you've felt consistently depressed for two weeks or more. Think of help for depression just as you would think of taking medicine for a cold or to stop a headache.

Some people think Christians shouldn't get depressed. After all, we have Christ as our Savior who can help us. What else do we need? This thinking can cause a lot of needless pain. Christians are humans, and sometimes humans just need a little extra help. And even Jesus felt similar emotions. When he was hanging on the cross dying, Jesus thought God had forsaken him. Jesus knew this was his mission and his purpose, yet in his pain, when he was distressed and depressed, Jesus cried out to God and asked why God had forsaken him (see Matthew 27:45-46).

From noon until three in the afternoon
darkness came over all the land.
About three in the afternoon
Jesus cried out in a loud voice,
"*Eli, Eli, lema sabachthani?*"
(which means "My God, my God,
why have you forsaken me?").

Matthew 27:45-46 (NIV)

We know how this story ends: Jesus went on to complete his mission and die on the cross for our sins. However, God raised him from the dead, proving that God is more powerful than death. But in the middle of the plan, while he was in pain, Jesus suffered, and Jesus asked God for help.

If you are depressed, cry out to God and to others you trust. Tell God and others exactly how you feel. There's hope and help available to you or someone you love who may be dealing with depression. Don't suffer alone—and don't allow others to, either. If you notice a friend is not herself or himself, say something. Offer your loving support and encourage your friend to get help, too. Read about ways to help and check in often with your friend.

For another take on depression in the Bible, read Psalm 42. How did David feel? What did he do about his condition?

During a time when you are not feeling low, write or record a list of ten things you enjoy doing. Review your list when you are down or depressed and push yourself to do one of the activities.

1. _____

2. _____

3. _____

4. _____

5. _____

6. _____

7. _____

8. _____

9. _____

10. _____

Whom can you talk to when you are feeling low? Prayerfully ask the Lord to show you trustworthy people in your life. Remember to be a listening ear for others.

MY GOD, MY GOD

Lord, thank you for caring about how I feel. Thank you for the people and resources you have given me to deal with my emotions. When I am down or depressed, remind me to cry out to you and to seek help. I know you love me and want the very best for me. Amen.

I Won't Let Anger Get the Best of Me

Just like depression, anger is an emotion that can be tricky. When you are angry, that emotion affects your thinking, or makes you feel like you're not in your right mind. If you make decisions while angry, chances are they will not be the choices you would make when you are calm, or when you're in your right mind.

So how should you handle anger? James 1 offers some good advice. The book of James is much like Proverbs—filled with wisdom. James 1:19 suggests we are to be slow to anger, meaning use all the willpower we have to stay in control and not get mad so quickly. Naturally, things will happen to make you angry. But if you can stop yourself from going straight to level ten every time something sets you off, you will be better able to handle things with a clear mind.

> Understand this, my dear brothers and sisters: You must all be quick to listen, slow to speak, and slow to get angry. Human anger does not produce the righteousness God desires. So get rid of all the filth and evil in your lives, and humbly accept the word God has planted in your hearts, for it has the power to save your souls.
>
> James 1:19-21 (NLT)

Think of it this way: If every time a frenemy says something about you that you don't like, you let her have it, you're allowing your frenemy to control you. If you decide to fight—whether with your fists or your words—when your ex-bestie whispers something as you walk by, you'll end up in more trouble than it is worth.

Learning not to lose it when you're hurt or mad takes self-control. And self-control is a good investment. It can help you remain calm and think clearly, rather than act rashly or recklessly. When you act rashly, you'll end up doing something you may very well regret later. And who has time for that?

Practice following James' advice: Listen quickly and think about all possible scenarios (is she really talking about you, could she just be jealous, or are you super sensitive?). Then take some time to think before you speak, or respond to what you think you heard or saw (be slow to speak). And then be even slower to get mad or angry (or react). Sitting back and trying to get a little perspective on a situation can go a long way. Try going for a walk, expressing yourself with a painting or drawing, or talking to a trusted confidant who can help you get a handle on the situation.

Write or record some things you can do to avoid letting your anger get the best of you, like dancing it out while blasting your favorite song. Review your list each day this week to help you the next time you are tempted to get angry.

Another good way to gain perspective on a situation is to ask yourself whether the issue will be important to you in one year. If it won't, it usually isn't that big of a deal. You can let it go and free your mind and your emotions for the important stuff.

PRINCE OF PEACE

Give me strength to resist getting angry about things that are unimportant. Help me practice listening more than I speak and gain the right perspective on things. Thank you for leading and guiding me. Amen.

I Want to Be Rich!

More than anything, Evie wanted to be rich and famous. She spent countless hours watching videos of her favorite stars. An avid follower of Beyoncé, the Kardashians, and Taylor Swift, she was fascinated with living the life. She wanted to be able to wear the nicest clothes from the hottest designers; she wanted her makeup to be on point every day and her hair to be done just right. She knew that in order to live her best life she needed to get rich.

Her mom and dad didn't have much money. They worked what she thought were dead-end jobs and struggled to pay the bills. They had just enough to provide the basics, or necessities, for Evie and her sister. Evie's mom told her daughters to be grateful for what they had, which would seem like a lot to some families.

Evie laughed at her mother when she said this. They barely had money; how could she be grateful? Evie had bigger plans. She'd make it to the top somehow—she was waiting to get discovered so she could secure the bag and get paid. She didn't want to be poor or even middle class. She wanted to be *rich*.

One day, all of those rich girls at her high school would see Evie on the screen; she'd be a model or an actress or married to someone famous. Then they'd want to talk to her and try to get in good with her. But she'd just look down on them like they looked down on her now. She would show them all.

Chasing money and fame can be a dangerous route; choosing a career just so you can make lots of money or become famous has led many people to live unhappy lives. Wanting money is fine; we all need money to provide for ourselves and our families. But wanting money more than anything is a red flag. If you find yourself feeling like Evie, give yourself a reality check now before you run into real trouble. The love of money leads to evil. Don't make getting money your main priority. It's a setup for failure and unhappiness.

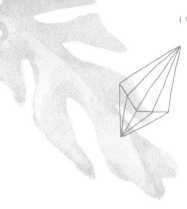

But godliness with contentment is great gain. For we brought nothing into the world, and we can take nothing out of it. But if we have food and clothing, we will be content with that. Those who want to get rich fall into temptation and a trap and into many foolish and harmful desires that plunge people into ruin and destruction. For the love of money is a root of all kinds of evil. Some people, eager for money, have wandered from the faith and pierced themselves with many griefs.

1 Timothy 6:6-10 (NIV)

To prevent yourself from getting caught up in wanting money more than anything, try naming your blessings. Gratitude is being thankful for what you have now. At the end of each day this week, write down or record at least five things you are grateful for.

Sunday

Monday

Tuesday

Wednesday

Thursday

_____

_____

_____

_____

_____

Friday

_____

_____

_____

_____

_____

Saturday

_____

_____

_____

_____

_____

_____

Think about how strongly money influences your thoughts about jobs or careers. Do you want to pursue a certain career only for financial gain? What else should motivate this important decision? Ask for God's guidance in your career choices and for managing money wisely, now and in the future.

GOD, MY PROVIDER

Give me a healthy perspective on money. Help me not love money more than I love Jesus or people. Help me be grateful for what I do have. Amen.

Girl Power

Women and girls have not always been treated fairly in society. Fortunately, things have changed quite a bit. Women are more empowered to choose the type of life they want to live. They do not have to fit into a box constructed by someone else.

Even when laws were not fair for women, some of them worked together to make changes. They had girl power before it was a popular saying. One such group of women is found right in the Bible in Numbers 27, the daughters of Zelophehad (or "Z" if it's easier!). These sisters—five of them—didn't have brothers, so when their father died, his land was going to be lost. They couldn't inherit it because the laws at that time didn't allow women to own land.

The daughters of Z didn't think this was fair, so they banded together and went straight to their leader, Moses, to ask for a change. Moses took their request to God, and God said they were right! The laws were changed because of their courage. These women didn't just sit quietly by and let this injustice go on. They stood up for themselves and brought about change. And that change helped women after them.

All girls and women—and boys and men, too—can gain a lot from studying the story of these powerful women. When you have courage to stand up for what is right for yourself and for others, you can change injustices. You can do what others consider impossible. It definitely takes courage and faith to ask for what you think is right. But when you believe deeply in a cause, you won't give up. You'll keep pushing and seeking justice no matter what. And an injustice doesn't have to be only about something affecting you or your

God ruled: "Zelophehad's daughters are right. Give them land as an inheritance among their father's relatives. Give them their father's inheritance."

Numbers 27:6-7 (MSG)

family; it can be something you think is unfair for someone else. God wants us to act justly (see Micah 6:8)!

Record or write a list of circumstances you think are unjust. What might you be able to do to fight these injustices?

Google organizations that are fighting against the injustices you have listed. How might you be able to partner with or assist these groups? Choose one activity to do this week.

MERCIFUL AND JUST GOD

Teach me how to courageously stand up for those who are being treated unjustly. Help me use girl power to impact this world. Amen.

When I Am Tired

Do you ever get tired? Just tired of schoolwork, of trying to juggle your schedule, of trying to fit in all the stuff you *want* to do and all the stuff your parents *expect* you to do? It's natural to get tired. Our bodies can only do so much before we need a break. Likewise, our spirits can need a break, too. And there's something much better than a super-powerful energy drink to help when we are weary and tired.

God has the power to energize us—physically and emotionally—when we need it. When we ask, God can renew our strength as we continue to run this race of life. By going to God, we acknowledge that we need God's help, that we don't want to do this thing called life alone. We want to rely on someone much stronger and smarter than we are. We want to allow God's supernatural strength to propel us, not just our human strength.

Isaiah 40:28 presents a great wake-up call to all of us trying to do life by our own strength and power. It's not possible. We are not strong enough. But God is. Almighty God is consistent and always available. God isn't human, so God doesn't tire out or need to stop and catch a breath.

God also knows everything—including how you're feeling and when you want to give up. So, if you reach out for help, God, who is sometimes called "the Comforter," knows and will give you exactly what you need to keep going (see John 14:26 KJV). God can help you feel fresh again and give you that extra pep you need in your step and inside your spirit.

Look to God, your Comforter, for renewal. Look to God for strength. God's got just what you need.

Don't you know anything?
Haven't you been listening?
God doesn't come and go. God *lasts*.
He's Creator of all you can see or imagine.
He doesn't get tired out,
doesn't pause to catch his breath.

And he knows *everything*, inside and out.
He energizes those who get tired,
gives fresh strength to dropouts.

For even young people tire and drop out,
young folk in their prime stumble and fall.

But those who wait upon God get fresh strength.
They spread their wings and soar like eagles,
They run and don't get tired,
they walk and don't lag behind.

Isaiah 40:28-31 (MSG)

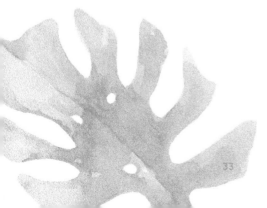

Write or record how you felt the last time you were exhausted physically and emotionally. How did you get more energy?

_____

_____

_____

This week, think of three ways you can remind yourself to turn to God for strength and renewal the next time you are tired.

1. _____

2. _____

3. _____

Take a walk and talk to God, and journal that conversation.

_____

_____

_____

The next time you are tired, try one of the activities you've listed. Compare how you felt turning to God versus doing what you did previously.

_____

_____

_____

EVERLASTING GOD

I know you do not get tired or need to catch your breath. You are amazing. I know I need to take a break sometimes and get renewed. Remind me to turn to you for strength. I know you are able and willing to help me keep going. Amen.

Get Moving

Physical fitness may seem like an odd topic when it comes to the Bible; however, God is concerned about our whole being—both spiritual and physical.

So, how's your fitness level? Is exercise for you only moving from car to couch? Do you cringe every time you hear the word "gym"? Don't worry, you don't have to try out for the track, gymnastics, tennis, or field hockey teams at school—although that's a great idea!—or train for a marathon, or become a CrossFit beast, to be fit. You can set your own standard for fitness based on your lifestyle and goals. But be clear, the Bible states that physical training has value (see 1 Timothy 4:8).

> For physical training is of some value, but godliness has value for all things, holding promise for both the present life and the life to come.
>
> 1 Timothy 4:8 (NIV)

To be physically fit or active can help you in many ways. It gives your body a fighting chance of staying healthy. An active body helps you think more clearly and avoid some diseases. When you feel your best physically, you can do your best—in school, in extracurricular activities, in the community, and at home. When you're at your best physically, you can accomplish more of your goals and help others with theirs.

> Do you not know that your bodies are temples of the Holy Spirit, who is in you, whom you have received from God? You are not your own; you were bought at a price. Therefore, honor God with your bodies.
>
> 1 Corinthians 6:19-20 (NIV)

Taking care of your body is another way of thanking God for it. Our bodies house God's Spirit; our bodies are the temple where God lives in us. We honor God by keeping our bodies healthy.

Good health includes being well physically (and mentally!). Eating good foods (like your veggies and fruit), drinking water, and exercising to the point of a comfortable, healthy sweat are ways to have good health. Find an activity that you enjoy and commit to doing it a few times a week: Try walking, biking, skating, dancing, or a sport. There's value in keeping fit.

Choose one or more physical activities that you enjoy and commit to doing them at least three times this week. List or record the activities you will try.

Throughout this week, pay special attention to what you eat. Keep a food journal and write down what you eat; circle the food choices that are healthy for you. Try to eat more of those items.

CREATOR

Thank you for being concerned about every part of me. I'm so thankful that you love me so much. Give me inspiration to stay fit and healthy as I take care of the body you have given me. Amen.

Let's Talk About . . .

"Let's talk about sex," says no one ever, except maybe your mom. It's awkward. But let's *talk* about those three little letters. Let's think *now*, before something happens. And sex *can* happen quickly, especially if you haven't really thought about your personal view on the subject or talked with your bae about your expectations. In a private place with your bae, after a few minutes of passionate kissing, it is probably going to be a little too late to bring up the subject of sex and follow through with your convictions. By that point your hormones—those powerful chemical messages from your body—will have taken over. It will be hard to even think straight. So why not think now—when your hormones and your body aren't pressuring your mind—about what you want to do when you're alone with your bae?

Because God is concerned about our whole being, the Bible says don't be immoral, or hook up with just anybody for sex. Your body is where God's Spirit lives. So sex is not only a body connection with someone; it's spiritual, too. The connection two people make during sex is designed to last forever.

> Don't you know that your bodies are part of the body of Christ? Is it right for me to join part of the body of Christ to a prostitute? No, it isn't! Don't you know that a man who does that becomes part of her body? The Scriptures say, "The two of them will be like one person." But anyone who is joined to the Lord is one in spirit with him. Don't be immoral in matters of sex. That is a sin against your own body in a way that no other sin is.
>
> 1 Corinthians 6:15-18 (CEV)

There's more to sex than mere skin on skin. Sex is as much spiritual mystery as physical fact. As written in Scripture, "The two become one." Since we want to become spiritually one with the Master, we must not pursue the kind of sex that avoids commitment and intimacy, leaving us lonelier than ever by separating us from God.

There is a sense in which sexual sins are different from all others. In sexual sin we violate the sacredness of our own bodies, these bodies that were made for God-given and God-modeled love, for "becoming one" with another.

1 Corinthians 6:16-18 (MSG)

You hurt God's Spirit, which is living in you, when you have sex, or enter into a "union," with someone you haven't committed to, someone you haven't taken vows to love and cherish forever. And you don't want to be connected *forever* to someone you may not even like tomorrow or next month! What you may feel for a special someone in a private moment, or feel about a relationship right now, isn't reason to make a sexual connection. You've heard it before, but the truth is God wants you to connect sexually once you're in a relationship that will last. We call that marriage.

Write down reasons to wait to have sex.

Who would make it easy to ignore your reasons not to have sex if you were kissing them in a private moment, and how could you bring up the subject with them before you both feel the urge?

_____

_____

_____

It's a good idea to think about just how far you want to go physically when dating someone. This week, think about whether the following acts are okay when dating: holding hands, kissing, touching, laying down together, and _____ (add your own actions).

Make a graph or use the example below to chart the activities you feel are okay and not okay to do before marriage. From left to right, write the activities, from the most to the least okay.

Then draw a horizontal line from the left to where your convictions say you will stop. When you are dating someone, review this chart together.

Write your thoughts on this below.

_____

_____

_____

Hand Holding	Lip Kissing	French Kissing	Sex

ALMIGHTY AND LOVING GOD

Help me manage my hormones when dating by truly knowing my boundaries before it's too late. Help me trust your timing, know my value, and allow only those who respect me to get close. I desire to honor my body and your Spirit in my body by _____

_____.

Amen.

Find True Love

Love is something most of us want in our lives. We see it in movies, we have an entire holiday devoted to exchanging love notes, and we often say how much we love something or someone.

Have you thought about what love is?

From what we see and hear around us, we think love is a feeling, but it is an action. The greatest example of love is God. God loves us unconditionally, meaning there is nothing we can be or do to make God *not* love us. Even when we ignore God or go against God's will, God loves us. That's true love.

First Corinthians 13 breaks down just what this true love looks like. We find this kind of love in God. As you read the scripture below, consider whether you find it in anyone else. Can you better demonstrate these actions toward the people you love?

Love is kind and patient,
never jealous, boastful,
proud, or rude.

Love isn't selfish
or quick tempered.

It doesn't keep a record
of wrongs that others do.

Love rejoices in the truth,
but not in evil.

Love is always supportive,
loyal, hopeful,
and trusting.

Love never fails!

1 Corinthians 13:4-8 (CEV)

Reread the scripture describing true love. Which traits do you have trouble demonstrating? Write them down or record them, and spend time praying about them this week.

_____

_____

_____

Think about a time someone you love has been kind, patient, not jealous, etc. Make a list of the characteristics of love from 1 Corinthians 13 and jot that person's name next to that item on the list. How did each example make you feel? Journal about your thoughts on love based on this scripture.

_____

_____

_____

LOVING GOD

Thank you for being my ultimate example of love. Show me how to love you like you love me and to love others the same way, too. Amen.

Show True Beauty

The right makeup, complete with lashes and gloss. Designer clothes. The perfect hairstyle. You get the look, right?

Well, the Bible has something to say even about beauty—our true beauty. God's Word says it isn't what we wear or how well our face is beat that's most important. Those things don't bring out our true beauty. They may make us look better in the mirror or help us conceal a blemish. But our true beauty comes from inside.

What does your inside look like? Is it filled with jealousy, ungratefulness, or bitterness? Does it show love, kindness, and joy—characteristics that God's Spirit produces in us (see Galatians 5:22-23)?

Makeup, clothes, and hairstyles can't cover up a bad attitude or ugly spirit. And the face of a beautiful spirit will always look pretty because it is connected to the ultimate Creator of beauty—God. The girl who receives strength and guidance from God, rather than relying on her looks, is beautiful, and she has peace even when life is harsh and cold. An inner gentleness is the type of beauty others want to be around. Godly beauty shares warmth like the rays from the sun.

> Your beauty should not come from outward adornment, such as elaborate hairstyles and the wearing of gold jewelry or fine clothes. Rather, it should be that of your inner self, the unfading beauty of a gentle and quiet spirit, which is of great worth in God's sight.
>
> 1 Peter 3:3-4 (NIV)

Go get beautiful. Connect with God for inner peace and share a little glow with the world.

Look in the mirror.

List your best physical features. Record or write your answer.

_____

_____

_____

List your best inner features.

_____

_____

_____

What can make you more beautiful inside?

_____

_____

_____

This week, think about what attracts you to a person. Reflect on whether those things are on your list of beauty features and write about it.

_____

_____

GOD OF ALL

Thank you for creating beauty all around me. I especially want to be beautiful on the inside and share your warmth and love with others. Give me a beautiful spirit that glows even in tough times. Amen.

But She's Different . . .

We live in a big world with many different people. Differences are all around us. Some differences are by choice—like choice of fashion styles and friends. Other differences are by birth or circumstances—like ethnicity and economic status.

Some people come from a different country or culture and have accents that make understanding them challenging. Others have hair and skin different from yours. Others learn differently.

Hopefully, you already realize that despite all of these differences, humans are alike in many ways, too. We all want to be safe and happy and to connect with family and friends.

But everyone definitely has times when our differences can get in the way of our connecting. What can we do at these times? One thing that can help is remembering that God is the Creator of all. Humans have plenty in common.

Another thing to keep in mind is to respect differences and try to understand where the other person is coming from. You don't have to agree with them, but try listening to their story or their viewpoint. You may learn something you didn't know. And life is much more interesting when you're open to discovering the unique gifts and cultures that others have to share—from stories to food to sports that could all be new and exciting to you.

Making judgments about a person or a group based on differences can lead to such negative, dangerous views and emotions as intolerance, prejudice, and hate. You'll be far better off without that negativity. Learn to love unconditionally like Christ did. Treat others with the same respect you'd like to receive, as Jesus instructed. It's the Golden Rule, after all.

> In everything do to others as you would have them do to you; for this is the law and the prophets.
>
> Matthew 7:12 (NRSV)

Read the story of Rahab in Joshua 2 and the story of the Israelites in Joshua 7:22-25. How was Rahab different from the Israelites? How did she help the Israelites? What reward did she receive?

Think of someone who is different than you are, or someone who might see you as different from them. List or record what you have learned from that person.

This week, pay attention to the differences between you and your classmates. Thank God for your differences and make an extra effort to treat everyone as you'd like to be treated. Write about your week in a journal.

DEAR GOD

It's me again. Thank you for all of the unique and amazing ways you've created people. Teach me to respect everyone and to treat them as I'd like to be treated. Amen.

Brothers and Sisters

Speaking of differences . . . sometimes no one seems more different than the people in your own home! Your brothers and sisters, or other young relatives in the house, can sometimes seem like aliens to you. How could you even be related? You like hanging out; she prefers staying in to read a book. You like shopping and finding great deals on cute clothes; he can literally wear the same shirt every day. You are neat and clean and organized; she can't find a thing in her room.

Accepting each other as we are—as the unique creations of God—can be harder when it comes to our family. Maybe it is because we live so closely together that we are more prone to get on each other's nerves. Perhaps because we're so close, our differences loom larger than others.

Whatever the reason, know that sibling differences are natural. And the same respect we give to others—to treat them as we'd like to be treated, no matter how different they seem—holds true for those in our family. We don't need to be alike to be loved and treated with kindness.

Siblings in the Bible had their differences. Look at Mary and Martha: One liked sitting at Jesus' feet and listening to his teaching. The other was more focused on providing food for Jesus and his entourage. Both seemed like good things to do. When Martha complained to Jesus, he reminded her to not worry about so many things.

We have differences. Chill. Just do you (and quit worrying about what your sister or brother is doing).

As Jesus and his disciples were on their way,
he came to a village where a woman
named Martha opened her home to him.
She had a sister called Mary,
who sat at the Lord's feet listening to what he said.
But Martha was distracted by all the
preparations that had to be made.
She came to him and asked,
"Lord, don't you care that my sister
has left me to do the work by myself?
Tell her to help me!"

"Martha, Martha," the Lord answered,
"you are worried and upset about many things,
but few things are needed—or indeed only one.
Mary has chosen what is better,
and it will not be taken away from her."

Luke 10:38-42 (NIV)

What differences have you noticed between you and other family members? Write or record them.

How can you focus on staying in your own lane this week and not worrying about the differences between you and family members? Write down some ideas and put them into action.

LORD, GOD

Thank you for creating me as me and my family members as who they are. Help me love them and treat them well in spite of our differences. Amen.

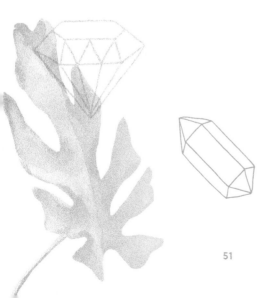

Friend to Friend

Want to be a good friend? The kind others can depend upon, and the type of girl people want to be around? There's one particular characteristic that can help: It's called empathy.

Empathy simply means you feel what the other person is feeling. If your friend fails a test, you feel for her; you hurt because she is hurting, because her GPA will probably drop. Another friend gets a car and makes everyone just a bit jealous. What do you do? You celebrate with her. You're happy because she's happy—not just because you're thinking of all of the places you want her to take you. Another friend loses a grandmother; you mourn with her and listen to her stories about her grandmother as she grieves.

Empathy is all about putting yourself, or at least your emotions, in the same place as the other person. Acknowledge what the other person is going through and simply say: "I am here for you; I may not have gone through what you have, but I am here to rejoice with you or mourn with you." Empathy says *I see you and I acknowledge how you are feeling. I want you to know I'm right here by your side—for all of it.* Empathy is not about you, but about the other person. It's putting their thoughts and feelings first.

Don't you wish everyone would use that special quality and show a little empathy?

> Rejoice with those who rejoice; mourn with those who mourn. Live in harmony with one another. Do not be proud, but be willing to associate with people of low position. Do not be conceited.
>
> **Romans 12:15-16 (NIV)**

Write or record a list of emotions you've felt through the week. Or make your list by drawing emojis. Reflect on how it feels to have someone empathize with your emotions.

_____

_____

_____

Pay special attention to the things your friends are enduring this week. Think of ways you can show empathy. Write down some ideas and put them into action.

_____

_____

_____

MY LORD AND MY GOD

Open my heart and mind and allow me to feel what my friends are going through. Remind me to rejoice with them when they are happy and to mourn with them when they are sad. Amen.

Finding and Giving Comfort

Losing a loved one to death is probably one of the toughest circumstances anyone faces. Whether it is a parent, a grandparent, a close relative, or a friend, saying good-bye for the rest of your earthly life is sad. Yet somehow, some way, those left on earth get through the loss of loved ones. Good memories provide needed comfort, reminding you of the times you shared and the moments you enjoyed. A friend might be there for you in an unexpected way.

God can also provide comfort. When you pray and ask, God can send what you need. God can help you manage your grief—the pain and sadness you feel inside—and help you get through it, even when you think it will be really hard.

Praise God, the Father of our Lord Jesus Christ! The Father is a merciful God, who always gives us comfort. He comforts us when we are in trouble, so that we can share that same comfort with others in trouble. We share in the terrible sufferings of Christ, but also in the wonderful comfort he gives.

2 Corinthians 1:3-5 (CEV)

Grief can also help you empathize with others. If you've experienced the sting of death and the loneliness you feel when grieving, you can better understand how hard it is for others who are dealing with loss. You can offer compassion and sympathy in a special way—because you have experienced a similar sadness. When a friend needs comforting, dig deep and recall how you felt and offer support. If you have not experienced loss, observe those around you who have and try to share the comfort you might like.

Think about some ways you would like to be comforted when grieving. Write down or record what might make you feel like someone cared. If you've experienced grief, you can recall the things others did that showed you they cared and how you felt.

_____

_____

_____

Here are some things NOT to say to someone grieving:

They're in a better place.

The good die young.

God calls the good home to be with Him.

There is a reason for everything.

They brought this on by . . .

You're not over it yet?

It was just his/her time.

Try to be strong.

Instead, say:

I am so sorry for your loss.

I wish I knew the right words to say; just know I care.

I am here to help in any way I can.

You will be in my thoughts and prayers.

I am just a phone call away.

Or just give a hug instead of saying anything.

Reach out this week to anyone you know experiencing grief. Do at least one of the things listed to provide comfort in their grief.

COMFORTING GOD

Thank you for promising to send comfort when I grieve. Remind me to rely on you to give what I need at the right time. Open my heart to share comfort with anyone who needs it right now.

What Am I Here For?

Finding your purpose. Pursuing your passion. Living out your purpose. These are all popular phrases. It seems as if everyone is looking for the meaning of life.

Knowing your purpose and following your passion matters, especially as you start to think about career choices. But purpose is much broader than just a job or even a hobby.

Purpose is why you are here on earth. It's big. It could take you all of your life to discover. Or you might find it early in life. You may also have more than one purpose and continue to develop them as you grow.

What's important is to realize that you do have a *purpose*. God designed you and placed you on earth for a reason—or reasons. That purpose is for good works. All of your purposes are for good works. You're not put here to harm others. You're not put here to harm the earth. No, you were made to do good.

Go ahead, take all the tests designed to help you find your passion or purpose. Try new things and discover what you enjoy doing. Listen to what others say you are good at. All may point to your purpose. But above all else, remember that your purpose will always lead you to do something good. Look for ways to do good and thank God for creating you to do good. The world needs the good work you do.

> For we are his workmanship, created in Christ Jesus for good works, which God prepared beforehand, that we should walk in them.
>
> Ephesians 2:10 (ESV)

Keep track of the things that you enjoy doing; write or record them. Make notes to describe how you feel when doing these activities.

_____

_____

_____

Reflect on how God may be able to use the things you enjoy doing as good works for others. How can these things point to your purpose in life? Write about it in your journal this week.

CREATIVE AND GOOD GOD

Thank you for creating me to do good works. I think my purpose may be to _____.
I look forward to discovering more about my purpose and what you have designed me to do. Amen.

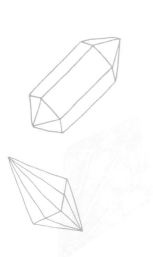

Using What I'm Good at for God

How do you treat those who have less than you, those who may be having a tough time?

Do you shake your head when you pass the homeless on the streets, thinking they should just get a job? Or do you have compassion for them, praying that things get better for them and offering help? Sharing money or food with the homeless isn't the only way to help. In fact, some people prefer to give money to organizations that help the homeless rather than giving it directly to a person—for safety and other reasons.

Consider volunteering with a group that supports a cause near and dear to your heart—helping orphans, single mothers, or disabled veterans. Plenty of organizations take care of people who are in need. Or you may write letters to officials seeking to change laws that would benefit the needy. Serving your neighbors—whatever way you choose to do it—is what God wants you to make part of your life.

When you take care of the hungry, or those who are thirsty, or those who are incarcerated, it is as if you are taking care of God. When you are kind to others and in service to them, you show God that you care about God's people, that you want to help those in need, that you recognize them as your brothers and sisters in Christ.

When you reach out to care, you reach out to God, too.

Then the king will say to those at his right hand,
"Come, you that are blessed by my Father,
inherit the kingdom prepared for you
from the foundation of the world;
for I was hungry and you gave me food,
I was thirsty and you gave me something to drink,
I was a stranger and you welcomed me,
I was naked and you gave me clothing,
I was sick and you took care of me,
I was in prison and you visited me."

Then the righteous will answer him,
"Lord, when was it that we saw
you hungry and gave you food,
or thirsty and gave you something to drink?

"And when was it that we saw you a stranger and
welcomed you, or naked and gave you clothing?"

"And when was it that we saw you sick
or in prison and visited you?"

And the king will answer them,
"Truly I tell you, just as you did it to one
of the least of these who are members
of my family, you did it to me."

Matthew 25:34-40 (NRSV)

Record or write your thoughts on serving those in need. How, specifically, have you helped?

_____

_____

_____

Open your eyes and look for someone in need. Who are they?

_____

_____

_____

List three ways you can help and reach out to someone this week, individually or with others.

_____

_____

_____

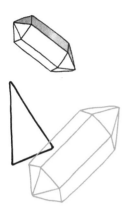

LOVING GOD

I want to serve you by helping others in need. Give me eyes to see when someone needs a helping hand and courage to assist. Amen.

Give Generously

God is generous and is pleased when we follow that example.

The Bible says giving is like farming. The farmer who plants plenty of seeds will have a large crop. The more seeds the farmer plants, the more crops the farmer reaps. When you want to hold on to stuff—money, time, and your gifts and skills—you end up like a farmer who doesn't plant much. You have a small crop. You may keep what you already have, what you won't let go of, but you won't reap much.

However, when you give, somehow you get more. When your hand is wide open and willing to share, you also seem to receive more in that open hand. It probably won't be from the same person you've given to, but you'll receive God's blessings in another way—perhaps even in the joy that giving to others brings. Giving shows God you are a good steward, or manager, and that you are able to handle more. God will care for you and keep you full as you help fill up others. It's a win-win. Give generously.

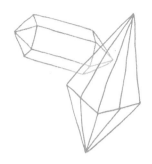

Remember this—a farmer who plants only a few seeds will get a small crop. But the one who plants generously will get a generous crop. You must each decide in your heart how much to give. And don't give reluctantly or in response to pressure. "For God loves a person who gives cheerfully." And God will generously provide all you need. Then you will always have everything you need and plenty left over to share with others. As the Scriptures say,

"They share freely and give generously to the poor. Their good deeds will be remembered forever."

For God is the one who provides seed for the farmer and then bread to eat. In the same way, he will provide and increase your resources and then produce a great harvest of generosity in you.

2 Corinthians 9:6-10 (NLT)

Record or write your thoughts about giving.

_____

_____

_____

List what you have given lately and to whom.

_____

_____

_____

List what you can give this week.

_____

_____

_____

Organize a give-a-thon. List what you and your friends can share with others, such as clothes, money, time, cleaning services, etc.

_____

_____

_____

Ask a few friends to join you in giving generously this week.

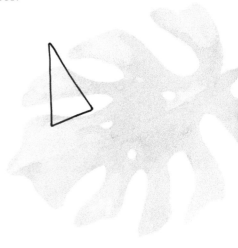

GIVING GOD

Thank you for being so generous to me. I want to follow in your footsteps and share with others. Give me the insight and courage to give freely. Amen.

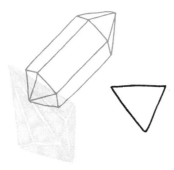

No-Bragging Zone

No one likes a braggart, a boaster. A girl who is always talking about herself. What she has done and what she has. "I'm all of that. I have the best of everything because I am the best—the greatest ever. Just call me perfect. Don't you wish you were me?"

Nope, that girl is no fun to be around.

At the root of bragging is insecurity—that ugly, self-doubting twin of boasting. When you don't feel good about yourself inside, you might feel the need to cover it up by bragging or boasting about yourself. You want others to think you are wonderful, even though you just might not feel that great.

There are cures for bragging and insecurity. Keeping your mouth shut is one, but another is to talk in a way that reminds you that you are created in God's image and God loves you—just as you are. There's no need to gain favor with humans by oversharing about how much you have and how much you've done. When you're not feeling your best, quietly ask God to help you see yourself as God sees you. Perhaps you'll get a reality check and realize you have a few things to work on, but you'll also be reminded that God's love is unconditional. No matter what, you're loved and you're enough.

> **Don't brag about tomorrow! Each day brings its own surprises. Don't brag about yourself— let others praise you.**
>
> **Proverbs 27:1-2 (CEV)**

And when you've done something praiseworthy, others will note it. Scripture says to "let others praise you." Receiving acknowledgment—without asking for it—will feel great. But if you don't get acknowledged for something you've done well, remember to acknowledge yourself to yourself and thank God—the giver of all good things (see James 1:17).

Record or write five things you can remember or say to yourself to stop you from boasting.

1. _____

2. _____

3. _____

4. _____

5. _____

When you are tempted to brag, check yourself by remembering one of those five things.

This week, practice praising others for things you notice they've done well or for their achievements. Take notes about how you feel complimenting others and how they respond to your genuine praise.

GIVER OF EVERY GOOD AND PERFECT GIFT

Thank you for my gifts. Even when I don't feel good about myself, I know that you love me and I am created in your goodness. I want to see myself as you see me. Amen.

Gossip Girl

Gossip is repeating or sharing information with someone who is not personally involved in the matter. If the matter involves only "person A," then telling "person B" or anyone else is gossip. If the matter involves "person A," and "person B" discusses it with anyone else, that is gossip. Even if it involves "person A" and "person B" only, and "person A" shared it with you, it's still gossip to talk about it with "person B." Godly communication is face to face, not about others.

Talking about others may seem like fun until you're the subject matter at hand. Girls who gossip can't be trusted. A girl may be talking to you about another person right now, but that means the tables may turn toward you eventually, since a friend who talks about one friend will talk about another friend, and eventually you.

Whether in person or on the phone or through social media, gossip is not cool. It's mean. It shows the gossiper's true colors.

Gossiping also includes listening to someone who is talking about others. It's almost as dangerous to be on the receiving end of gossip. If you listen, you're participating—even if you don't join in the talk. Your willingness to take in the information keeps the gossiper going; it affirms her. She wouldn't be talking if she didn't have an audience. The best way to avoid listening to gossip is to stop the talker midsentence with "I don't need to know whatever you're about to say," and then change the subject. If the person continues in the same vein, exit the space, end the conversation, or unfollow the thread.

Without wood a fire goes out; without a gossip a quarrel dies down.

Proverbs 26:20 (NIV)

The way to avoid participating in gossip—talking as well as listening—is to check yourself. Just as boasting and insecurity go together, so does gossiping. It is also a part of that duo. When you talk negatively about others or betray others' secrets, you are seeking notoriety, popularity, or to take the attention off yourself. When you are not feeling your best, you might easily find yourself gossiping or enjoying listening to gossip or following it on social media. Ask yourself: "What is going on with me? Do I feel proud of myself or happy with where I am?" If not, decide to make changes in yourself. And start by not betraying a friend's confidence or sharing your opinion about her with others. Working on yourself is a good way to combat the need for gossiping.

Think about the times you've told or listened to gossip. Write down how you felt.

_____

_____

_____

Go on a fast from gossiping. That means to take it out of your diet. Don't listen to it and don't share it. Keep your lips sealed and ears closed to any negative talk about others this week. Track how you overcome this temptation in a journal by writing about each time you avoid gossip this week.

_____

_____

_____

LORD, GOD

Show me how to keep my mouth shut and my ears closed to gossip. Fill me with thoughts of good things and ways I can be better. Amen.

Power Words

We know guns and knives can kill, but words can be deadly, too. Words have power. They can either encourage and inspire or kill someone's spirit. Something inside—in our spirit and will—suffers when negative words are spoken to us. Words can lead to the death of desires and dreams.

When you say mean things—to someone's face or behind her back, even jokingly—it can damage the person. He may hear them and begin to believe them, too. She may feel inner pain and be crushed. He may see himself differently, which can lead to him acting differently. Her self-esteem can be damaged. Who he is destined to become can be stunted.

> Words kill, words give life; they're either poison or fruit—you choose.
>
> Proverbs 18:21 (MSG)

However, when you say words that are kind and encouraging, you may actually help someone live a better life. You may inspire someone to keep going when it's tough, or to gain optimism. Your good words can lift a head on a low day. They can give hope and life.

Your own words can have the same impact on you. When you say things to yourself that are negative—"I can't do it," "I'll never be good," "I don't deserve good things"—you create a mental trap for yourself. These negative thoughts spoken to yourself can lead to more negative thinking and then to negative actions.

Words of life are what we all need: "I can do all things through God's power" (see Philippians 4:13). "I am loved" (see John 3:16).

Let your words give life to yourself and others.

> The tongue has the power of life and death, and those who love it will eat its fruit.
>
> Proverbs 18:21 (NIV)

Record or write five positive words or phrases to inspire yourself.

1. _____

2. _____

3. _____

4. _____

5. _____

Make a point to share encouraging and inspirational words with friends this week. Consider creating a word picture using several words to describe them. You can make these online or draw your own. (See wordart.com, worditout.com, or a similar site.)

GOD OF LIFE

Help my words share life with others and with myself. Show me how to inspire and encourage those around me and myself through what I choose to say or not to say. Amen.

My Thought Life

The brain is powerful. It's where thoughts are housed, and thoughts often impact actions. As a man thinketh, so he does, says Proverbs 23:7. As a woman thinketh, so she does, too! That means that what you think guides what you do. Cleaning up your thought life will help you live your best life.

Thinking you can do a task increases your chances of success. Thinking you can't do it will help you fail. Thinking you are an original creation from God will help you do amazing things, because, since God created you, you're *good*, and because you belong to God, you have the Almighty's *help*.

Doubting yourself is, in essence, doubting God. That can lead you to not even try very hard. You count yourself out before you give your best.

Thinking negatively about past situations can make you see the worst possibilities; things may not be as bad as the image of your circumstances you've conjured in your mind. Spending time in prayer and reading God's Word can influence your thoughts to focus on the positive and help you rely on God's strength, not just your own.

And now, dear brothers and sisters, one final thing.
Fix your thoughts on what is true, and honorable,
and right, and pure, and lovely, and admirable. Think
about things that are excellent and worthy of praise.
Keep putting into practice all you learned
and received from me—everything you
heard from me and saw me doing.
Then the God of peace will be with you.

Philippians 4:8-9 (NLT)

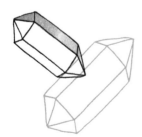

Read the scripture. Write down or record three things in your life that are:

True

1.

2.

3.

Honorable

1.

2.

3.

Right

1.

2.

3.

Pure

1.

2.

3.

Lovely

1.

2.

3.

Admirable

1.

2.

3.

This week, think about the things you have listed. Be intentional about focusing on these things. Expect more peace as you think on these things.

GOD MOST HIGH

I love you and all you are. Keep my mind focused on you and all that is worthy of praise. I want my mind to lead me into joy and peace. Amen.

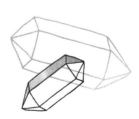

Doing My Best

I have to admit, sometimes I am jealous of my friends, even my bestie. She always seems to get good grades, and everyone likes her. She is really nice. I just want to be as smart and popular as she is, but I'm not. I'm an average student, and people seem to like me when I'm with her, not because they want to be around me. It's tough being friends with someone who seems so perfect.

If you've ever thought like this girl, this scripture might give you some perspective. It's odd because it comes from the story about Cain and Abel, two brothers in the book of Genesis, chapter 4. Verses 6 and 7 speak to this kind of thinking. Read the words God spoke to Cain, who was mad because his brother Abel's offering was accepted by God but his wasn't. Sound like you and your friend? Ask yourself honestly: "Why am I mad—because she gets good grades and is popular? Have I done the hard work I need to do to get good grades?" If you're honest, your answer might be "No. I don't like to study as much as I need to, and quite frankly, I don't like people nearly as much as my friend does." This Bible passage reminds you to do your best—whatever that is for you, not for your bestie.

Time passed.
Cain brought an offering to God
from the produce of his farm.
Abel also brought an offering,
but from the firstborn animals of his herd,
choice cuts of meat. God liked Abel and his offering,
but Cain and his offering didn't get his approval.
Cain lost his temper and went into a sulk.

God spoke to Cain: "Why this tantrum?
Why the sulking? If you do well,
won't you be accepted? And if you don't do well,
sin is lying in wait for you, ready to pounce;
it's out to get you, you've got to master it."

Genesis 4:3-7 (MSG)

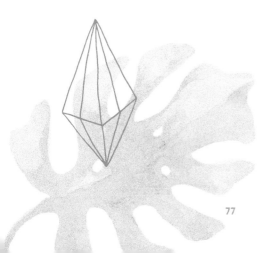

Now, instead of negative self-talk, like in the opening example, you might try a perspective like this:

"I need to make sure I've given my all to my work. I will not compare myself to her or anyone else. I'm not racing against anyone. I need to be my best self. Period. Then I will be happy with my results, and I think God will be, too. Doing Me. Being Me. That's what's up. That's what I need—to be my best self."

Think about what you need to do to be your best. Write or record five thoughts and five actions that will help you be your best self.

Thoughts that will help me be my best self:

1.

2.

3.

4.

5.

Actions that will help me be my best self:

1.

2.

3.

4.

5.

Read the story about Cain and Abel in Genesis 4:1-16. What messages do you get from this story that you can apply to your life?

_____

_____

_____

What hashtags would you use to describe this story?

_____

_____

_____

GOD OF ALL

I want to be my best self. I don't want to compare myself to others. Give me the wisdom and determination to be *me* and do my best without comparing myself to anyone else. Amen.

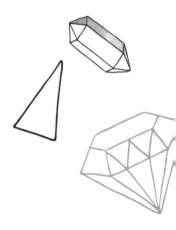

The Beauty of Patience

"Patience is a virtue" is an old cliché with great value, not only because patience is an admirable quality, but because it is one of the qualities Christians develop when they are growing in the Spirit of God. The Bible calls these qualities "fruit of the Spirit" (see Galatians 5:22). When God lives in us and guides us, one of the characteristics we display is patience.

Patience means we can put up with unpleasant stuff without letting it get the best of us, and we hang in there when things seem to take a very, very long time. We don't clap back easily at those who insult us. We don't rush a process when it is taking longer than we expect. We wait with a good attitude, knowing that God is in the mix, and at some point, things will change. We wait for that time with anticipation and with optimism.

Waiting is not fun. Never, ever is waiting fun. But those who've developed the virtue of patience can keep calm while they wait. They focus more on the sweet end result, rather than the painful or boring or seemingly never-ending current process. Patience prevents them from making rash moves and often helps them gain understanding.

Impatience can make you jump the gun and make a decision that, in the end, will be unhelpful. Wait optimistically. See the difference a dash of patience will make in your life.

> Whoever is patient has great understanding,
> but one who is quick-tempered displays folly.
>
> Proverbs 14:29 (NIV)

In what three areas do you need to exercise more patience? Record or write them down, as well as your plans to be more patient.

Areas where I need more patience

Plans to be more patient

1.

1.

2.

2.

3.

3.

Patience is encouraged throughout the Bible. Use a concordance or an online Bible to search for the word "patient" or "patience." List seven passages about patience here, one for each day of the week:

1.

2.

3.

4.

5.

6.

7.

Read a passage every day this week and recall them when you need to add a little more patience in a situation.

HOLY ONE

Give me patience. I want to wait with a good attitude, so I can gain great understanding. Thank you for being so patient with me. Amen.

Discover Discipline

Does the word "discipline" bring to mind something that resembles punishment—what happens to you when your parents take away your cell phone because you got low grades or stayed out later than curfew? The word "discipline" originally meant "to teach," and it's actually a way to get you to see that you need to do better. The serious message translated through discipline is meant to help you correct your wrong behavior.

Your parents may seem harsh and unreasonable, but when you realize the only reason they have rules is to protect you, and they discipline you for breaking those rules, you can understand their discipline is also protecting you. If they didn't care about your well-being, they could let you stay out all night and get bad grades. But because they have rules, and discipline you when you don't follow them, this shows that they do care about you and want the best for you.

Parents are actually imitating God when they provide discipline. When we have to endure the consequences of our wrongdoing, God is correcting us and showing us that God cares too much for us not to let us learn the lesson we need. God knows better than we do what we will encounter down the road, and what we are being prepared for. Discipline helps establish rules and healthy boundaries inside us, so when we're on our own, we follow them when nobody is looking, although nobody makes us.

Self-discipline is sacrificing yourself and putting in hard work to attain a goal. You might need discipline to learn a foreign language, to play an instrument, or to compete in a race. You set your goal and practice to achieve it. You set milestones that help you reach your goals and make commitments to meet them. You sacrifice time and let go of other things that get in the way of your goal.

Whether meant to benefit our external or internal selves, discipline makes us better. We all need it sometimes.

God is educating you; that's why you must never drop out. He's treating you as dear children. This trouble you're in isn't punishment; it's *training*, the normal experience of children. Only irresponsible parents leave children to fend for themselves. Would you prefer an irresponsible God? We respect our own parents for training and not spoiling us, so why not embrace God's training so we can truly *live*? While we were children, our parents did what *seemed* best to them. But God is doing what *is* best for us, training us to live God's Holy best. At the time, discipline isn't much fun. It always feels like it's going against the grain. Later, of course, it pays off handsomely, for it's the well-trained who find themselves mature in their relationship with God.

Hebrews 12:7-11 (MSG)

What can you do to embrace discipline as correction and as an important characteristic in helping you meet goals?

_____

_____

_____

List one goal you need discipline to accomplish. If it is a big goal, write several milestones you will need to reach before getting to the goal. Write a mantra or phrase that you can repeat each day this week to help you commit to reaching your goal or milestones.

_____

_____

_____

LOVING GOD

Thank you for caring enough about me to discipline me when I need it. I want to apply discipline in my life to reach the goal of

_____.

Give me what it takes to be disciplined and meet my goal. Amen.

When I Am Afraid

Make this journal entry your own by filling in the blanks:

If I'm honest, sometimes fear creeps in at the most inconvenient of times. Right when I think I have enough talent, skill, or courage to _____ (audition for the big show), I hear a voice saying I am not good enough or I can't do it. I cringe when I remember the time I wanted to say hello to _____ (someone I admired), but my words wouldn't come out. Or when I really wanted to apply for the _____ (special program at school), but when I looked at my grades, I thought, "I'll never make it."

Fear has stopped me from doing what I secretly want to do. I haven't told even my bestie some of my dreams and goals, because I just don't think they will happen for a girl like me. My dreams seem too big and too unlikely at times.

I've found the recipe for being happy whether full or hungry, hands full or hands empty. Whatever I have, wherever I am, I can make it through anything in the One who makes me who I am. I don't mean that your help didn't mean a lot to me—it did. It was a beautiful thing that you came alongside me in my troubles.

Philippians 4:12–14 (MSG)

But at other times, I have a moment of clarity. I recall that fear is not of God. It's not how God operates or wants me to operate. God doesn't make me scared and fearful. No, trusting in God gives me power and faith and belief that I can do what I put my mind to; I can do what I desire to do with practice and hard work. I am disciplined enough to go after my goals and get things done. Maybe not because I'm so awesome, but because with God, I can gain strength to do all things.

I need to remember to rely on God when fear tries to creep into my mind. I don't have time to let fear stand in my way of going after what I'm designed to do. Fear can't stop me. I use my faith to push fear out of my mind and go for it.

> For God did not give us a spirit of cowardice, but rather a spirit of power and of love and of self-discipline.
>
> **2 Timothy 1:7 (NRSV)**

Times I allowed fear to stop me from pursuing a goal or dream:

_____

_____

_____

An old phrase made an acronym for fear: Fake Evidence Appearing Real. Fear is made up in the mind. It makes things appear real, when they really are not. Memorize this acronym this week or make up your own about fear. Use it to help you overcome the feeling of fear the next time you experience it, and don't let fear prevent you from pursuing any more goals or dreams!

ALMIGHTY GOD

I'm so thankful to know you've not given me the spirit of fear. I don't want fear to stop me from moving forward and pursuing goals. Replace my fear with power, love, and self-discipline. Amen.

God Is Faithful

One of the most beautiful and comforting aspects of God is faithfulness. To be faithful means to do exactly what you say you will do, to keep your word, to be reliable and dependable. God is faithful.

Make this affirmation, by reading it aloud:

I am called to be faithful, too. When I say I will show up and help out, I show up and help out. When I say I will follow up with an item or detail, I do it. I am my word. What I say is what I do . . . most times. I'm not as dependable as God, but I do try and aspire to be faithful. My friends and my parents know they can count on me to do what I say I'm going to do and be where I say I'm going to be.

When I falter, I ask for forgiveness and try to make it up. When I know I can't be faithful, I give enough notice so my unfaithfulness will cause as little disruption as possible.

Being faithful is not easy for me. Sometimes I just don't feel like doing what I've committed to do—or something better pops up. It is at these times I especially appreciate God's faithfulness. I'm very happy that I can count on God. I can depend on God's love, which is always there and unchanging and unwavering. God is there for me each day, just like the sun rises and sets. I can depend on God. God is faithful.

The steadfast love of the Lord never ceases,
his mercies never come to an end;
they are new every morning;
great is your faithfulness.

Lamentations 3:22-23 (NRSV)

Think about what it means to be faithful. List people you know who are faithful. Write or record reasons why you think they are faithful.

_____

_____

_____

How does it make you feel when someone is faithful to you? Journal about your thoughts this week and write how you will be more faithful to God and to others.

FAITHFUL GOD

I am so happy I can depend on you. I am so grateful for your faithfulness. It makes me feel _____.
I desire to be faithful to you and to others. Amen.

Kind God

A teen girl heard a song on the radio saying that God is kind, and she was shocked. For some reason, she thought of God as a tyrant who is constantly looking to see when we mess up. She thought of God as big and powerful, knowing and seeing everything that we and others do. She thought of God as a judge who hands down verdicts and punishments when we are wrong. But she never thought of God as kind.

Are you that girl?

Do something solitary that just feels good and peaceful—take a walk in the park, go for a swim, draw, knit, crochet, or color. Imagine God with you, enjoying the activity, and begin to think of God as kind as you make this affirmation aloud:

God, who is larger than life and all-powerful, is also kind to me. God created me, provides for me, and sent Christ for me. Wow! God is kind, and kind to me. I've had a small view of who God is. God isn't mean or strict. God's rules are not to punish me but to make me better, to keep me safe, and to help me make it through this life. God is indeed kind to me.

> But when the kindness and love of God our Savior appeared, he saved us, not because of righteous things we had done, but because of his mercy. He saved us through the washing of rebirth and renewal by the Holy Spirit, whom he poured out on us generously through Jesus Christ our Savior, so that, having been justified by his grace, we might become heirs having the hope of eternal life.
>
> Titus 3:4-7 (NIV)

If you've ever had a teacher or coach who you thought was mean and strict, write why you felt that way. (For example, she made us do more homework than any other teacher.)

_____

_____

_____

Now write how you felt the next year or a few years later. (For example, when I went to the next grade, I was really prepared. I did well in my classes because of how that teacher had prepared me. What I thought was mean was actually good for me.)

_____

_____

_____

Write or record some words that express who God is for you. (For example, kind, mean, powerful, etc.)

_____

_____

_____

Read or listen to the lyrics of the song "Kind God" by Marvin Sapp or another praise and worship song you like. What do the lyrics say about God? Do you agree or disagree? Why? Write your thoughts in a journal.

KIND GOD

Thank you for caring about me and being kind to me. Open my eyes so that I can see more of who you really are.

When I Pray

Prayer used to scare me. It sounded so serious and religious. If it scares you, too, or feels strange, know that you're not alone.

But, once I heard that prayer is simply speaking to God, I began to talk to God just like I talk to a friend or my mom or someone else I trust. Prayer connected me to God, and now it feels like God has been my best, longest, lifetime friend.

An acronym helped me learn to pray. It is called ACTS. Each letter represents a different part of prayer, just like the "hello," "good-bye," or other parts of conversations with friends.

A stands for Adoration, meaning I spend time thinking of God's amazing qualities and adoring God when I begin to pray.

C is for Confession; I confess anything I've done wrong or I've neglected to do recently. I don't want sin or wrongdoing to get in the way of my relationship with God, so I confess it and ask for forgiveness.

T stands for Thanksgiving. I have a lot to be thankful for, and I know everything good comes from God, so I spend time in prayer thanking God.

S is supplication, which means I ask God for what I want. I pray for my needs and the needs of others.

It helps to use this short word ACTS to remember to include all these parts in my prayer.

But sometimes I'm moving too quickly for all that, and I just cry out to God, "Help me!" This lets God know I need something right now. "Show me what to do" and "Jesus, take the wheel," meaning control this situation, are other short prayers I whisper to God frequently. Or I'll say, "Awesome, God!" when I want to give God a high-five that something amazing happened. Talk to God more often to keep your connection strong.

This, then, is how you should pray:
"Our Father in heaven,
hallowed be your name,
your kingdom come,
your will be done,
on earth as it is in heaven.
Give us today our daily bread.
And forgive us our debts,
as we also have forgiven our debtors.
And lead us not into temptation,
but deliver us from the evil one."

Matthew 6:9-13 (NIV)

Write or record a prayer using the ACTS model.

_____

_____

_____

_____

_____

_____

Read the Lord's Prayer from Matthew 6:9-13. Identify the different parts of ACTS in the prayer. You can use a dictionary or different versions of the Bible for words you may not understand. Repeat the Lord's Prayer each day this week.

HEAVENLY FATHER

I adore you because _____. I confess that I have _____ and I want you to forgive me. Thank you for _____. I want you to give me _____ and help _____. Amen.

What Will Heaven Be Like?

Those who accept Jesus Christ as Savior are promised eternal life (see John 3:16 and John 10:10). Heaven is considered the place where we will ultimately live eternally with God.

Revelation, the last book of the Bible, shares a vision of what Heaven will be like. The descriptions of Heaven in Revelation are metaphors and may seem confusing, but the images can bring comfort and give us something spectacular to look forward to.

Revelation 21 gives us an idea of what will happen in Heaven:

Earth, as we know it, will not be. There will be a new earth and a new Heaven. (v. 1)

God will be right there with us. (v. 3)

Pain will not exist in Heaven. (v. 4)

Death, grief, sorrow, or anything else that's negative will not exist. (v. 4)

We will have no reason to cry. What makes us sad and unhappy now in this life and on this earth will no longer exist. Our hurts will be swallowed up and will not come back. (vv. 4-5)

We will have total peace and joy. (v. 6)

When life gets you down, reflect on God's promise of Heaven. Imagine living without sorrow or pain. Heaven is definitely something to look forward to.

Then I saw "a new heaven and a new earth," for the first heaven and the first earth had passed away, and there was no longer any sea. I saw the Holy City, the new Jerusalem, coming down out of heaven from God, prepared as a bride beautifully dressed for her husband. And I heard a loud voice from the throne saying, "Look! God's dwelling place is now among the people, and he will dwell with them. They will be his people, and God himself will be with them and be their God. 'He will wipe every tear from their eyes. There will be no more death' or mourning or crying or pain, for the old order of things has passed away."

Revelation 21:1-4 (NIV)

Write down or record things that make you feel:

Earth is damaged _____

God seems far away _____

Pain _____

Grief _____

Sorrow _____

Like crying _____

Unhappy _____

Hurt _____

Spend time this week thinking about Heaven. Read some of the promises found in Revelation (like 21:1-4; 21:15-21; 21:22-27; 22:1-5). Then cross out each of your answers and next to each crossed out answer write down how you think it will feel to be in Heaven with no more pain or sorrow.

_____

_____

_____

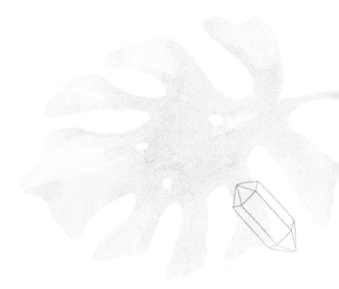

HOLY GOD

I thank you for your promise of eternal life in Heaven. I look forward to living with you forever and living in perfect peace. When life is tough, remind me of your promises, so I may continue in faith to look forward to eternal life. Amen.

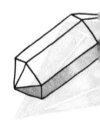

No Shame in the Game

Shame grabbed hold of me like wet clothing, tough to peel off or discard. I allowed shame to cling to me—instead of letting my shame go—thinking it was all my fault. I shouldn't have been there. I shouldn't have spoken up or said anything to anyone. I should not have.

I absorbed all of the blame for what happened, and I allowed shame to live within my mind and heart for a very long time. It even followed me to bed at night, often taking over my thoughts and causing me to toss and turn without sleep. When I did manage to shut off the thoughts and fall asleep, my dreams replayed the incident over and over. Those nightmares—reliving it all over again—forced me awake, in fear.

Shame made me cut off my closest friends. They would never understand. If they ever found out what happened, they wouldn't want to be my friends. Maybe they already knew. Did everyone figure it out? The stares made me think they knew.

I figured my mom would yell and scream and then make me do something I didn't want to do. It was easier to carry the weight of my shame than to talk to her.

I kept it to myself, carried my shame everywhere, and allowed it to remind me that I was no good.

Shame is a complicated emotion. It can make you feel worse the longer you keep it secret. If you are a victim of shame, you will discover freedom by believing and trusting in God.

The book of Isaiah shows how God restored Israel and how Jesus restored Christian believers to God. Being released from shame is a gift of God. Mercy—the way we are released from shame—is part of the character, the personality of God. Exchange despair and inner sadness for peace with yourself and true gladness. Give God your shame.

The Spirit of the Lord God
has taken control of me!
The Lord has chosen and sent me
to tell the oppressed
the good news,
to heal the brokenhearted,
and to announce freedom
for prisoners and captives.
This is the year
when the Lord God
will show kindness to us
and punish our enemies.
The Lord has sent me
to comfort those who mourn,
especially in Jerusalem.
He sent me to give them flowers
in place of their sorrow,
olive oil in place of tears,
and joyous praise
in place of broken hearts.
They will be called
"Trees of Justice,"
planted by the Lord
to honor his name.

Isaiah 61:1-3 (CEV)

Are you carrying around any shame? Write or record your thoughts on what is causing you to feel shame.

_____

_____

_____

As you read the verses in Isaiah 61:1-3, picture receiving flowers to replace sorrow. Draw a picture of flowers next to what you wrote. Put a small bunch of fresh flowers in your room this week. Each time you see the flowers, thank God for taking away your shame.

With whom could you trust and confidentially share what you wrote?

_____

_____

_____

Share this message with someone who may need to let their shame go.

_____

_____

_____

HOLY GOD

Thank you for taking away my shame. When it tries to creep back into my mind and cause me to feel ashamed again, remind me that you have given me flowers for my sorrow. I will not let shame take over my life. Amen.

God Knows My Name

Does God seem distant at times? Like some unknown being far away, unconcerned with you and the details of your life?

That couldn't be further from the truth. God *is* the great Creator of everything and the Almighty who powers all life, yet God is present with you and knows you and all the seemingly minor details of your life. God knows what bothers you or worries you or makes you excited. God knows you and wants to relate to you intimately. God *cares* about you.

Imagine how mothers feel about their babies. God is, beyond imagination, greater than a mother. God cares for us better than the best mother ever could. God knows our names. A scripture in Isaiah says our names are written on the back of God's hand. Our names are right there for God to see!

God knows you and God cares about you, so why not talk to God about how you're feeling? God cares enough to listen and to help. Reflect on how it feels that God knows your name and all about you. Write or record your thoughts.

How much do you know about God? Write down what you know and what you'd like to know. Look for answers in your Bible or talk to a Christian you trust to help you find the answers.

"Can a mother forget the infant at her breast,
walk away from the baby she bore?
But even if mothers forget,
I'd never forget you—never.
Look, I've written your names on the backs of
my hands.
The walls you're rebuilding are never out of my sight.
Your builders are faster than your wreckers.
The demolition crews are gone for good.
Look up, look around, look well!
See them all gathering, coming to you?
As sure as I am the living God"—God's Decree—
"you're going to put them on like so much jewelry,
you're going to use them to dress up like a bride."

Isaiah 49:15-18 (MSG)

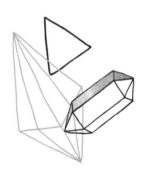

KNOWING GOD

I am comforted knowing that you know me. Thank you for knowing and loving me. I want to talk to you about everything, especially _____. Give me guidance in this situation and the courage to follow you. Amen.

Speak Up

If you're anything like me, when you were little you were told not to tattle. When my mom or teacher got tired of me running to tell who had hit whom on the playground or cut in front of me in line, I was told to stop tattling and to mind my own business. I learned to just be quiet and stay in my lane.

But when is it best to speak up? To intervene? Where is the line between tattling and saying what needs to be said?

Which response fits you?

"When I see someone being treated unfairly, I speak up. It's not right, and I'll intervene to try to get a bully to just stop. I've walked right up to a bully and told her to leave a girl alone."

"I've told my mom, my teachers, my youth leaders, and others when I've witnessed someone picking on a helpless victim. It's not always popular, but I think it is right. I share exactly what I've seen and let them deal with it."

"I've discovered my voice when others pick on me. I might look shy, but I speak up for myself."

> Have I not commanded you? Be strong and courageous. Do not be afraid; do not be discouraged, for the Lord your God will be with you wherever you go.
>
> Joshua 1:9 (NIV)

"If I don't think something is right, I say so. Sometimes things change, other times they don't, and I just walk away. But I speak up."

"I'm learning to speak up when I need to; it could save someone's life."

"I'm learning to like using my voice."

Write or record about a time you spoke up for yourself or someone else, or write or record about a time someone spoke up for you. How did you feel in either situation?

This week, ask family and friends to describe moments when they have spoken up for themselves or someone else. Ask them how they felt. Then make a list of the tips and ideas they give you on speaking up. Refer to the list whenever you have to speak up.

Tips and ideas on speaking up:

ALMIGHTY GOD

Give me the strength and the courage to speak up when I need to. Give me wisdom to know when my voice is needed. Thank you for giving me a voice, a mind, and a heart to protect myself and others. Amen.

When I Am Anxious

Anxiety is the worst. It has sneaked up on me at the oddest times. Everything can be going great, and I'm looking forward to something like a big party with friends or an interview for a summer job. Then boom. Anxiety hits. I feel overwhelmed and almost paralyzed. The thing I was looking forward to now scares me. I imagine all sorts of worst-case scenarios, and I can't seem to get past them. My heart races. My hands get all sweaty just thinking about what could happen. The sad part is that if my anxiety shows up, I'm certain to cancel my plan, although it was something I wanted, something I was looking forward to. But I just can't move past those thoughts and feelings that I'll show up and make a fool of myself. I hate the feelings I get with anxiety.

Anxiety doesn't have to get the best of you. Talk to someone you trust—a friend or a therapist—in combination with the Bible's prescription for anxiety, which is to talk to God. Pray all the time, about everything, says 1 Thessalonians 5:17.

> Do not be anxious about anything, but in every situation, by prayer and petition, with thanksgiving, present your requests to God.
>
> **Philippians 4:6 (NIV)**

When you have a big event coming up, start praying about it as early as you can. Ask God to give you peace. When you feel anxiety creeping up on you, stop and whisper a prayer. Give thanks for the power of prayer as you tell God what you need. It works and will help you release anxiety and live your best life.

Think of a time you've felt anxious or worried about a situation. Write or record how you felt.

_____

_____

_____

Start a gratitude journal or gratitude list this week. Each night before bedtime, write several things you are grateful for. Thank God for each of them throughout the week. You may want to continue the list after the week is over. Thanksgiving is a great way to focus on what you have rather than what might happen, which causes anxiety.

DEAR GOD

It's me again. Give me peace and calm when anxiety creeps into my mind. Teach me to focus on you and your power instead of what could or could not happen. I'm thankful for all you have done, and I will list my blessings instead of worrying. I thank you for _____. Amen.

Meet the Holy Spirit

Although I have several good friends, sometimes I get lonely. Even in a crowd, I can feel all alone, like no one really understands me, that if I dropped out of the crowd, no one would notice that I was gone.

I don't like being lonely; it is so isolating. It makes me feel sad. When I was little, I used to pretend I had a twin sister who liked everything I liked and enjoyed what I did. We'd play together and talk about our feelings. Pretending was fun, but I'm too old for that now.

If you love me, show it by doing what I've told you. I will talk to the Father, and he'll provide you another Friend so that you will always have someone with you. This Friend is the Spirit of Truth. The godless world can't take him in because it doesn't have eyes to see him, doesn't know what to look for. But you know him already because he has been staying with you, and will even be *in* you!

John 14:15-17 (MSG)

When Jesus was on earth, he made a promise to his followers. Jesus promised to send a friend to all who would believe and follow him. That friend is the Holy Spirit. You can't see the Spirit, and you can't touch the Spirit, but the Spirit can live in you, and you can feel the presence of the Spirit. You can talk to the Spirit and ask for guidance and company. You can rely on the Spirit to show you the right way and to warn you when there's danger. The Spirit is God. God is right there with you. God's Spirit can be your constant and real friend. You don't have to be lonely or alone—God is with you.

Write or record how you feel when you are alone.

List several things you do to try to not feel lonely.

Be aware of God's presence this week. Talk to the Holy Spirit often. Reflect on how you feel knowing God is with you.

HOLY SPIRIT

Walk with me and guide me as you promised in your Word. Help me get to know you better and be comfortable in your presence each and every moment of my day. Amen.

All Things Can Work Together

I love to bake cookies. I started baking cookies with my grandma when I was a little girl. I loved hanging out in the kitchen with her because it would be just the two of us. I felt like I got all of my grandma's love and attention when we were in her kitchen.

Now I like baking cookies even when I'm not at grandma's house and I'm at my house alone. It reminds me of my grandma's love, but it is also relaxing. I have my own mixer that my grandma gave me, and I've tried all sorts of cookies—peanut butter, sugar, chocolate chip, and my favorite, peanut butter double chocolate chip. My friends often ask me to bring them cookies. One friend suggested I try starting my own little cookie business and selling them. I'm not sure about that, but making money does sound like a good idea.

When I'm baking, I normally taste each of my ingredients as I mix them into the bowl: sugar, flour, chocolate, butter, chocolate chips, etc. I like to make sure everything is fresh.

But nothing beats the taste of warm cookies straight from the oven. They are the best. It's funny how each ingredient alone doesn't taste nearly as good as all of those yummy items mixed together and put under heat for 20 minutes.

The final product always reminds me of one of my favorite scriptures, "All things work together for good for those who love the Lord!" (Romans 8:28 my translation). Every moment may not seem good alone, but somehow and some way, God works it out and works it together to make something awesome.

> We are assured and know that [God being a partner in their labor] all things work together and are [fitting into a plan] for good to and for those who love God and are called according to [His] design and purpose.
>
> **Romans 8:28 (AMPC)**

Write or record your thoughts about Romans 8:28. Do you think all things work together for good? Why or why not?

_____

_____

_____

This week, bake your favorite cookie or treat. Taste each ingredient separately and then taste the finished product. Reflect on moments in your life where things came together and tasted good—much better than they seemed when you were encountering them separately or individually (like the ingredients).

_____

_____

_____

CREATIVE GOD

Thank you for weaving different parts of my life together to produce goodness. Give me the faith to know that even things that don't seem good can be used for my good. Amen.

Shine Brightly

A famous quote—attributed to several different people—says: "Don't curse the dark, light a candle." This isn't a verse in the Bible, but it could be.

Throughout scripture, Jesus uses the image of light to describe both his followers and himself. If we say we love God and want to follow Jesus' teaching and ways, then we, too, are called to be lights. That means we are to shine brightly, especially in darkness.

How do we shine? We live as examples of love, joy, peace, and justice. When there's darkness—something ugly like evil, hatred, or cheating—we don't give into the dark; we turn on our lights and shine. We show others how to find goodness, how to love instead of hate, and how to work hard and play fairly, rather than cut corners and cheat. By our examples, we are the light.

Darkness can be scary; it is very hard to see when it is dark. But light can make a big difference in times of darkness. Light can help others see a better path. Be the light for others to make their way through darkness. Shine brightly.

> You are the light of the world. A town built on a hill cannot be hidden. Neither do people light a lamp and put it under a bowl. Instead they put it on its stand, and it gives light to everyone in the house. In the same way, let your light shine before others, that they may see your good deeds and glorify your Father in heaven.
>
> Matthew 5:14-16 (NIV)

List or record several ways you can be light in dark situations around you.

_____

_____

_____

Get a flashlight or use a flashlight app on your phone. Light it up each night as you pray to God, asking to be shown how to shine brightly in the dark situations you face.

GOD OF LIGHT

I want to be a light that sits on a hill and shines brightly in the dark. Help me not give into darkness but remember to light my candle and shine brightly. Amen.

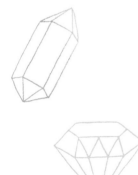

I Am a Witness

Think back to the court cases you've seen on TV shows or the news. A witness is vitally important in a court case. A witness gives testimony to what she has seen or heard. Witnesses are needed to verify what happened.

Witnesses for God are needed in our world. Witnesses for God help others see how Christians act as they follow Jesus. They show God's love in everyday life.

Are you prepared to be a witness for God? Could someone tell you are a follower of Christ just by how you treat others? Are you able to share in a few sentences the message of Christ? What would you say if a friend asked you *why* you are a Christian?

Your best witnessing can come through your actions—the love you demonstrate, your fairness, and the peace you reflect in trying situations. Your actions may cause people to ask questions: "Why are you not worried?" "Why are you hopeful and optimistic?" "What made you help that person who's not one of us?" Those are your openings to be a witness for God.

Practice now sharing how you would tell someone about God. Prepare your elevator speech— a message short enough, yet complete enough, to get your point across on a quick elevator ride.

> Let the peace of Christ rule in your hearts, since as members of one body you were called to peace. And be thankful. Let the message of Christ dwell among you richly as you teach and admonish one another with all wisdom through psalms, hymns, and songs from the Spirit, singing to God with gratitude in your hearts. And whatever you do, whether in word or deed, do it all in the name of the Lord Jesus, giving thanks to God the Father through him.
>
> Colossians 3:15-17 (NIV)

Write or record your elevator speech about why you are
a Christian.

_____

_____

_____

Practice it with another Christian and ask for feedback, so you'll
be ready to witness for God when the situation calls for it.

Find a song that shares the story of Christ and add it to your
playlist. Be ready to share it with someone this week.

GOD, MY LORD AND SAVIOR

**Thank you for loving me so much. I want to share your good news
with others. Show me how. Amen.**

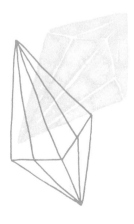

Don't Quit

Everyone has thought about quitting something: piano lessons, gymnastics, school! When things get challenging, boring, or monotonous, a natural reaction is to want to call it quits.

But unless you're talking about letting go of unhealthy habits or relationships (yep, those are best to quit), quitting doesn't accomplish anything. But when it is something that will benefit you in the long run, you can take these steps *before* quitting to help you make the best decisions.

Take a break before making a decision to quit. If you want to quit after a particularly long day or hard lesson, wait. Don't make the decision to quit when you're tired. Instead, get some good rest and see how you feel in the morning. Rest does the body good, and it also clears the mind.

If you still want to quit after a good rest, talk to someone you trust. Explain why you started *and* why you want to quit. Look at both reasons and ask the trusted person to help you gain perspective on the situation.

Consider whether you need to change something—like your practice schedule or workload—rather than quit. Look for another, less drastic solution.

Remember, there are always rewards for finishing a course. You will feel accomplished. The Bible says you will reap what you sow. Check out Galatians 6:7. What you do will come back to you. Your hard work on those grueling lessons will pay off if you hold out and finish the course. Keep doing your best and depending on God. Don't quit and never give up, because God will give you strength to finish!

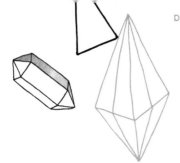

[God] gives strength to those who are tired.
He gives power to those who are weak.
Even young people become worn out and get tired.
Even the best of them trip and fall.
But those who trust in the Lord
will receive new strength.
They will fly as high as eagles.
They will run and not get tired.
They will walk and not grow weak.

Isaiah 40:29-31 (NIRV)

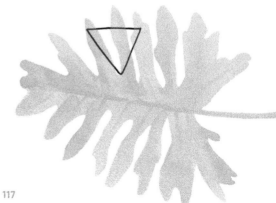

Write or record about how you felt in a situation where you wanted to give up or quit.

_____

_____

_____

Write about how you felt after you made a decision not to give up, but instead finished a difficult or challenging task.

Three things I didn't reap when I gave up

1. _____

2. _____

3. _____

Three things I learned when I didn't give up

1. _____

2. _____

3. _____

Review your reflections this week to prepare you for the next time you think about quitting. Write a mantra, or short phrase, to remind you not to quit.

_____

_____

_____

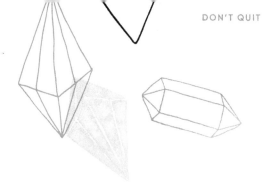

ALMIGHTY GOD

I get tired and discouraged sometimes. I need you to renew my strength and give me a determined attitude. Help me not quit but keep going. Amen.

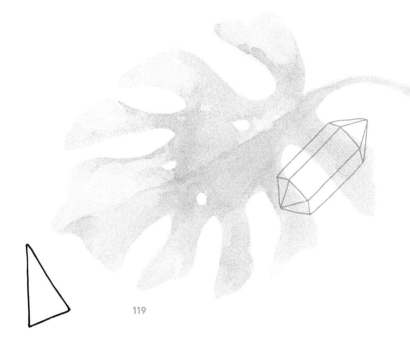

A Good Friend

When I was younger, a teacher told my mom she liked the relationship I had with my BFF. The teacher told my mom that we brought out the best in each other. While I was shy and often reserved, my friend was outspoken and adventurous. My BFF drew me out of my shell, and I helped her focus. We helped each other— in good ways.

That girl and I are still cool 'til this day. We go to different high schools, so we don't see each other often, but I still think of her when I'm choosing friends, especially close friends. My friend taught me to choose friends who will influence me in positive ways. She never tried to change me, but because we were good friends, she made me want to be a little more like her and try different things. I showed her the importance of settling down and getting your schoolwork done.

Considering whether someone could be a good friend, or deciding to invest in a relationship, is something to take seriously. If that girl or boy doesn't bring out good things in you or make you want to be better, it's usually better to pass on becoming closer friends. Aim to align yourself with good people around you and those who want good things from you. That's what friendship is all about.

You're going to need good people around you when times get rough and you need extra encouragement. You'll be glad to know you have friends who will have your back and support you in becoming your best. You can do the same for them, too.

Friends always show their love. What are relatives for if not to share trouble?

Proverbs 17:17 (GNT)

List your close friends. Write or record one reason why they are your good friends.

My good friends   **Why this friend is good for me**

_____   _____

_____   _____

_____   _____

This week, share how you feel with your good friends. Write them a note, send them a special text, or make them a gift to show you appreciate their friendship.

HOLY GOD

Thank you for blessing me with good friends. Help me be a good friend, too. Give me courage to set boundaries with people who are not good friends. Amen.

Getting My Way

Fill in the blanks to make this your personal statement:

Everyone wants their own way. It's how people are wired (James 4:1-2). I _____ (my name) am no different. I know what I want and when I want it. I even know exactly how much I want. I'm pretty focused like that. (Smile!)

But I've learned from God, the Bible, and other Christians that there's a better way to live. I'm learning that what I want to do and my plans may not be what's best for me. And I'm okay with that.

I'm learning to have faith and to trust and believe that God will work everything out. And when God does, I will have more than I want, and all of my needs will be met. God knows better than I do.

And that's what two of my favorite verses say. I need to do what God says to do first. I need to make God my priority. I need to make doing what God says a priority. The rest will flow from there.

But more than anything else, put God's work first.
Do what God wants.
Then the other things will be yours as well.

Matthew 6:33 (CEV)

Take delight in the Lord,
and he will give you the desires of your heart.

Psalm 37:4 (NIV)

These verses remind me to be happy knowing God, relating to God, and before I know it, God will give me what I want. God already knows what I want. God also knows how to make me want what's best for me. What I desire will be given to me, or God will change what I desire.

I think I'm getting this Christian lifestyle after all. I'm going to keep growing and learning to find out more! God makes this life worth living.

What God wants you to do:

_____

_____

_____

What you want that you trust God will give you:

_____

_____

_____

Look in your closet and list items you haven't worn or used in a while. Think back to when you *wanted* those items. List them and gather them up to donate to a charity or give to others.

Items I wanted but don't want anymore:

_____

_____

Reflect on God's wisdom in not giving you what you want, knowing what is best for you and that sometimes those wants are temporary.

HOLY GOD

I believe you make my life worth living. I desire to know more about you and grow closer to you. Show me how to put you first in my life. Amen.

The Power of Encouragement

Finding your gift—or wondering what in the world you were put here for—can be a daunting task. I used to look at my friends and see their gifts so easily—one acts really well and will probably be on Broadway or in Hollywood one day. Another can sing like a bird. I go to school with a lot of really smart kids, who will probably end up being CEOs or doctors or lawyers. They can easily use their gifts in good jobs, to help people or make life better for all of us.

But me, I feel pretty average. I don't stand out in anything. I study hard and get my work done, but I don't make all A's and I know I won't score the highest on any test. Ever.

My cousin once told me I was a good encourager. She said whenever she feels down, she knows she can just message me for a chat, and I will get right back to her with some uplifting words. My bestie told me that, too. She said I can see the best in every situation, and I speak up to share what I see. I do see good in people, and I hate to see them down or discouraged.

Sharing your thoughts to help uplift people is a gift. It may not always seem as important as some other gifts, but how would people get any of those seemingly more important tasks done if they didn't have some kind of encouragement? Even the smartest and most talented person needs encouragement. Whatever your gift may be—even if it seems very small and somewhat insignificant—it is important, and it can be used to help others. Use the gift you've been given. Develop and nurture it so you can do it well, excellently. You have a gift. Now go out and use it.

> Therefore encourage one another and build one another up, just as you are doing.
>
> **1 Thessalonians 5:11 (ESV)**

Read about Deborah in Judges 4:1–10. How did she serve as an encourager to Barak? What did she say? What did she do?

_____

_____

_____

What are some ways you can encourage your friends and family members this week? Write or record some ideas.

_____

_____

_____

Make a point to encourage those around you this week by selecting at least five people from your list; uplift them this week.

GOD, MY FRIEND

I want to be an encourager to others. Show me who needs to be uplifted. Please give me the words to say or actions to take that will encourage and uplift that person. Amen.

The Gift of Hospitality

Another gift people can overlook is hospitality. Hospitality is how you make people feel when they come into your home, school, community, church, etc. It's how you make a new person or visitor feel in your environment. It doesn't have to be at your home. Wherever you are, when you make people feel comfortable or welcome, you are being hospitable.

If you've ever been the new girl in any situation—at school, on the team, at camp, at church, in a family or friend situation—you know it can feel weird. You're not sure how things are done. You may not know anyone's name, where the bathroom is, or where to put your belongings. A person with the gift of hospitality would sense that you are getting used to this new space and help you out. She would show you what to do, invite you to come along, and just look out for you.

The only thing that counts in showing hospitality is that you care about people and want to help them get adjusted. You don't take it for granted that a new person will just figure it out. You take it upon yourself to make sure the newcomer feels welcomed and comfortable in the new environment.

Hospitality can go a long way in making a difference in someone's day—or life. By being a friend to someone who needs one, you just may get a chance to welcome that person into the Christian faith. Through your warmth and hospitality, they may want to know more about what makes you so joyful and hopeful. Your actions could spark their interest in knowing Christ.

Most important of all, you must sincerely love each other, because love wipes away many sins.

Welcome people into your home and don't grumble about it.

Each of you has been blessed with one of God's many wonderful gifts to be used in the service of others. So use your gift well. If you have the gift of speaking, preach God's message. If you have the gift of helping others, do it with the strength that God supplies. Everything should be done in a way that will bring honor to God because of Jesus Christ, who is glorious and powerful forever. Amen.

1 Peter 4:8-11 (CEV)

Read about Lydia in Acts 16:11–15. How did she show hospitality? How can you make other people feel comfortable? Write or record your thoughts.

_____

_____

_____

Read 1 Corinthians 12 this week. Think more about your gift. How can you use it to help others?

_____

_____

_____

Be on the lookout this week for "new" people. Show hospitality by making them feel included.

LOVING GOD

I want to follow your example, to show love to everyone, and to make others feel welcomed. Give me eyes to see when someone needs help and a heart to reach out to others in love. Amen.

When I Act with Integrity

Ever since I was young, my mother preached about "integrity." She said I needed to have integrity—to do what I know is right even when no one is looking. She said integrity would carry me a long way. I had no idea what she was talking about until I met someone who lacked integrity.

I went to school with a girl I thought was really nice. She was beautiful, and she always seemed to treat people well. She smiled a lot and had good friends. She and I became good friends, and when I started hanging out with her more, I noticed a pattern.

This girl was all smiles and good when people were watching— especially people she wanted to impress, like our teachers and other adults. But when she was just with me, she was very different. One time, we were in a department store, and she stole a pair of shades. Just put them on her face and walked out. I followed her outside and said, "I have some money. I could buy these for you." To my surprise, she replied, "I have money, too, but no one was looking, so why not take them?" She said she knew the security system at that store, since she shopped there a lot, and those glasses didn't have a security tab that would set off an alarm. She was right.

This girl, my former friend, did some other things that made me realize what my mom was talking about. When no one but I was looking, she was not who she was in front of others.

Integrity means you act as the same person, with the same character, whether or not someone is looking. If you say you believe stealing is wrong, you won't steal—even if you could do it without getting caught. No, your internal compass guides you to follow what you know is right. That's integrity. Not everyone lives with integrity, but you can!

Honesty lives confident and carefree,
but Shifty is sure to be exposed.

Proverbs 10:9 (MSG)

Read about the Bible character Job (pronunciation rhymes with the word globe) in Job, chapter 1. You can also read other chapters such as Job 2 or Job 38-40. How did Job show integrity?

Think of people you know who have integrity. What makes you name them? Write or record your thoughts.

GOD, MY SAVIOR

Please help me to live with integrity, to do what is right no matter what pressures I face. Give me wisdom, strength, and courage to follow you in every circumstance. Amen.

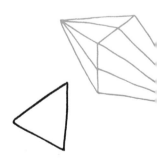

When a Little Is a Lot

I used to think I'd wait until I was older, perhaps rich and maybe even famous, to do good. I wrote in my journal about all of the great organizations I'd donate money to, and I made up names for a few groups I'd like to start. I could be a philanthropist like the people I read about or see on TV or in videos. They dig deep and give scholarships, donations, etc. I really admire those people.

I still do admire them, but a story in the Bible made me look at my giving differently.

Sitting across from the offering box, he was observing how the crowd tossed money in for the collection. Many of the rich were making large contributions. One poor widow came up and put in two small coins—a measly two cents. Jesus called his disciples over and said, "The truth is that this poor widow gave more to the collection than all the others put together. All the others gave what they'll never miss; she gave extravagantly what she couldn't afford—she gave her all."

Mark 12:41-44 (MSG)

When the rich people gave lots of money, it seemed great. Poor people depended on those offerings. But then the story went on to say Jesus honored the offering of a poor woman he observed giving two small coins. This woman was a widow. Women depended solely on men to take care of their financial needs during that time, so since her husband was dead, she probably didn't have any income. She gave two cents in the offering, while others gave much more. Jesus was touched by her gift because it was all she had. Her two cents counted more than what the rich people gave. They had plenty and only gave a tiny portion of what they had. This woman had very little and gave her last two cents.

You don't need a big bank account or lots of stuff to share what you do have. You can do what seems small right now with your money, time, and ideas. Right now. You don't have to wait to have more. You can share now.

List what you have to share:

Money _____

Time _____

Experience _____

Other _____

This week, what ways can you share what you listed with others?

_____

_____

_____

GIVING GOD

Show me how to be generous with what I have. Remind me not to wait until I have more to share. Amen.

I Don't Have to Worry!

In today's world, there's a lot to worry about. From the big stuff—like senseless violence and clean water—to the smaller stuff (that can seem big!)—like making good grades and having enough money to buy the outfit your mom refuses to get for you. Each day can bring something new to fret over and worry about.

But there's a way you can handle all those concerns—turn them over to God. Yes, you can give your concerns to God by praying. Pray about what is bothering you or causing you to worry. Leave that issue with God, knowing God hears each of your prayers and will answer in God's own time.

Anxiety doesn't have to be a way of life; worries need not occupy your mind. You don't need to try to figure out every detail about tomorrow. There's a better way to live.

God delights in handling our problems. Scripture says the Lord wants to hear from you and wants you to share your worries. Why? Because God cares for you. Yes, you. "God cares for you, so turn all your worries over to [God]" (1 Peter 5:7).

God wants you to surrender your concerns. God cares enough to take your concerns and work things out for you. You can be carefree.

So go ahead, follow the scripture and turn your worries over to God, who is waiting to hear from you. God cares enough to take away your worry.

Life is better and more fun when you release worry and surrender control. God's got you and God cares for you. Rest in the beauty and security of God's care—and don't worry.

God cares for me. I don't have to worry. I can turn everything over to my great God.

> God cares for you, so turn all your worries over to [God].
>
> 1 Peter 5:7 (CEV)

Write down everything that concerns you.

_____

_____

_____

Then say a prayer, releasing the issues to God. Keep track of how these issues are resolved by writing down what happens next to the problem. Write the date things are resolved, too.

Read how Hannah handled her concern in 1 Samuel 1:1-11. What was her issue? What did she do? Then read 1 Samuel 1:19-20 to see what happened.

Write down or record what you will do every time you begin to worry.

_____

_____

_____

Read 1 Peter 5:7, for example, then pray, write a letter to God about your concern, etc. Review your plan every day this week.

ALMIGHTY LORD

Thank you for caring so much for me that you want me to turn my worries over to you. I ask that you _____.
I release this issue to you and anticipate your answer.

God Loves Me

I used to go to church every Sunday with my grandma. She was the only one in my family who went to church. My mom and dad said they weren't into religion. My grandma took me with her, and I liked church when I was younger. I stopped going after I got older.

One Bible verse I remember from those times and often think about is John 3:16: "God so loved the world that he gave his only Son, so that everyone who believes in him may not perish but may have eternal life." As a kid, I had to memorize that scripture. I can still remember it all of these years later.

One day, I was sitting on my bed, and I thought of this scripture. For the first time, I let it sink in. God. Loves. Me. I got a few chills thinking about that. Wow.

I've looked for love for most of my life—probably since my grandma died. I've wanted to feel loved. I wanted to know someone liked me and cared for me and wanted to be with me. And that day on my bed, I realized that God loves and cares for me and wants to be in a relationship with me. God wants me to do what I'd do with a human friend—talk, share, care. It's already what God does for me.

For God so loved the world that he gave his only Son, so that everyone who believes in him may not perish but may have eternal life.

John 3:16 (NRSV)

Of course, having human friends and loved ones is important. We all want to feel connected to those around us. But you can count on God's love to never change. It is forever.

Write or record the names of the people you love and why.

_____

_____

_____

Write how it feels to know God loves you.

_____

_____

_____

LOVING AND CARING GOD

Thank you for loving me so much that you gave Jesus for me. I want to live my life thanking you for your love and your gift of eternal life. Amen.

Live Well!

Those who believe in Jesus have been promised eternal life (see Romans 10:13). We have a guarantee of living with God forever. Death will not be final for us. We will live with God.

But there's also another promise that comes with God's gift of Jesus—it's an abundant life. That's the life we can live right now. Christians who have accepted the gift of Christ and believe in all God has promised live differently. They live with joy and peace and happiness. They live abundantly.

Yes, we have issues. Yes, we have challenges and problems. But when you see them in light of all that God can do, has done, and will do, those issues look different. We have the power of prayer, and we turn to God with our issues. Our hurt or anxiety or worry doesn't last. We trust and hope in God. We look for God to help us handle our situation or to change it so we can meet adversity, anticipating that God will help us handle it. We can live abundantly—knowing we have much in this life and in the life after this.

> I came that they may have life, and have it abundantly.
>
> John 10:10 (NRSV)

I will live abundantly.

Reflect on your life. How abundantly do you live? Write or record your thoughts.

Live abundantly! Make a commitment to turn to God in prayer when you meet a challenge this week. And share the good times with God, too, through praise.

MY GOD, MY SAVIOR

I thank you for all you've promised me and all you've done for me. I desire to live the abundant life you've given me until I live with you eternally. Show me how to enjoy this life. Amen.

INDEX OF TOPICS

BIBLICAL CITATIONS

ACKNOWLEDGMENTS

I offer special thanks to God for the gift of writing and the opportunities to share this gift with others, especially teen girls.

I thank my family for always giving me the time and space to write. I love you, Derrick and Kayla.

I am grateful for my friendship and professional relationship with my editor, Adrienne Ingrum. To the team at Callisto: Wesley Chiu, Holly Haydash, Gary Clark, Andrew Yackira, and Melissa Valentine.

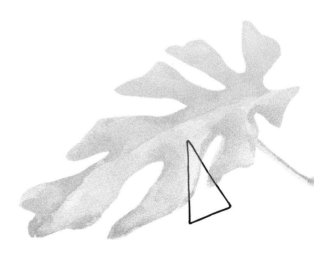

ABOUT THE AUTHOR

Katara Washington Patton is an author, editor, and speaker who enjoys sharing with all of God's people, but especially teen girls. She is a wife and mother who lives in Chicago, Illinois. Find out about her other books at Katara.PattonHome.net.

CPSIA information can be obtained
at www.ICGtesting.com
Printed in the USA
LVHW050724221020
669411LV00005B/7